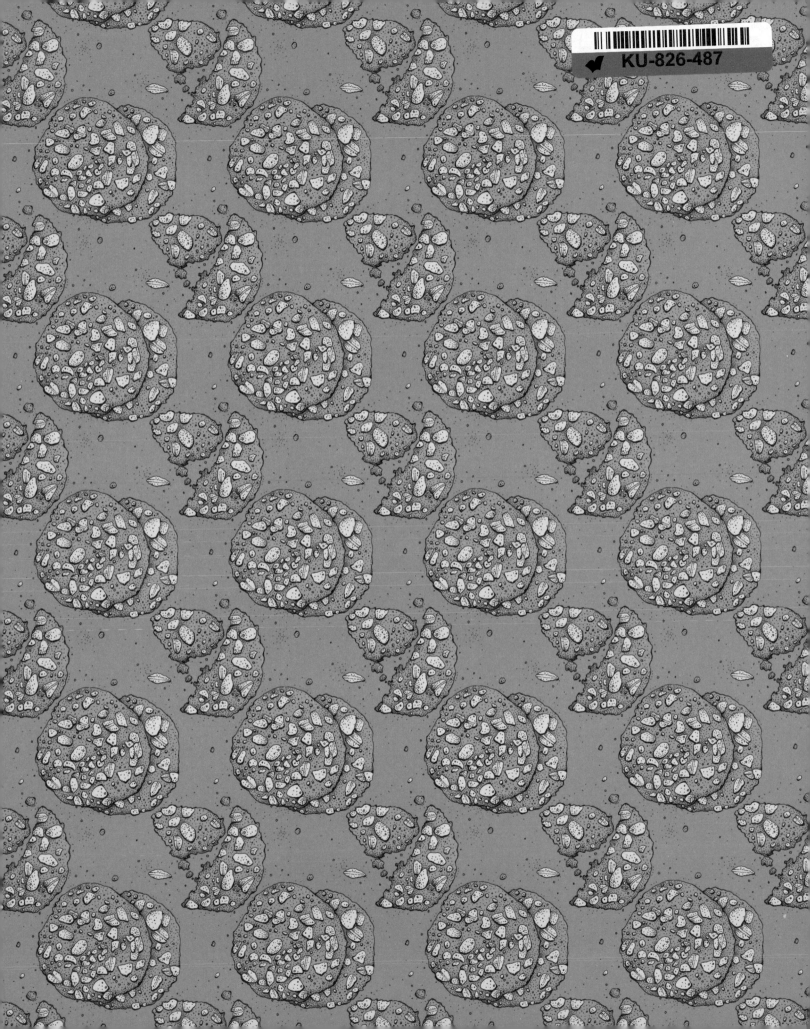

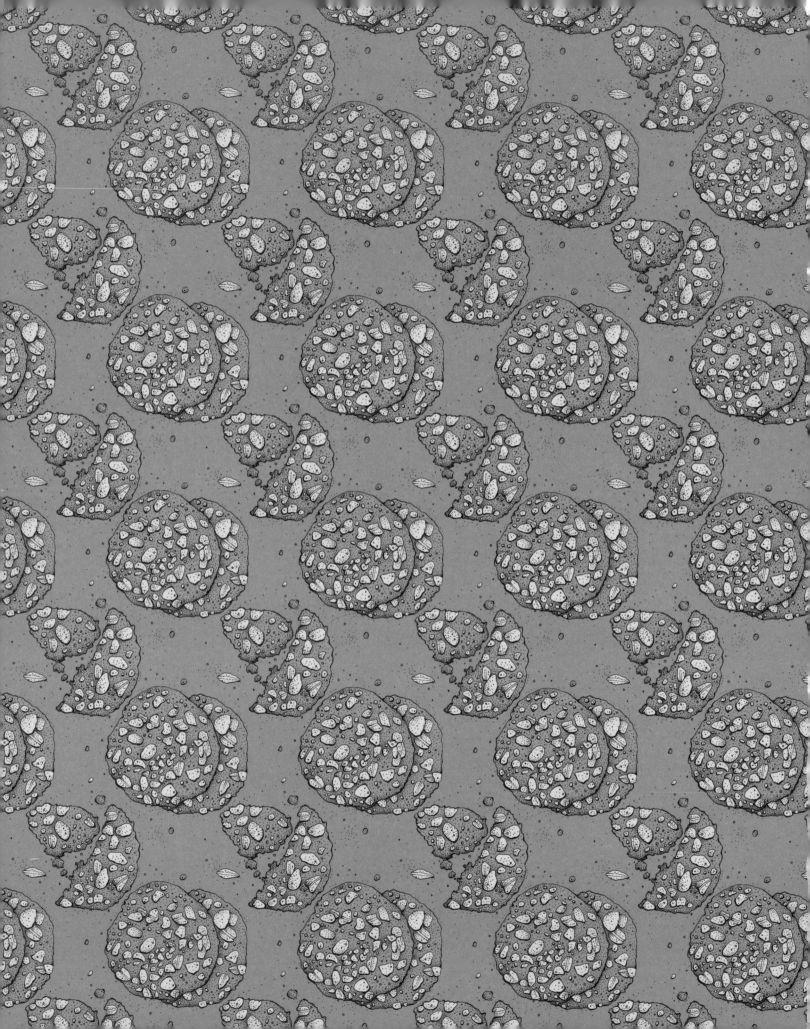

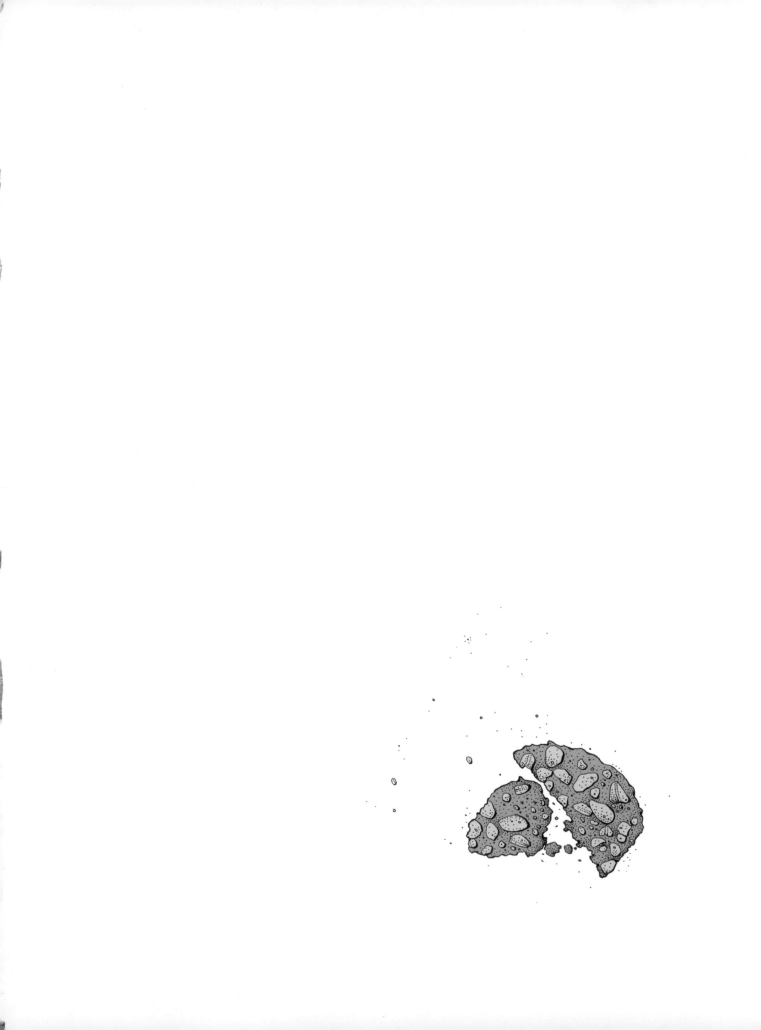

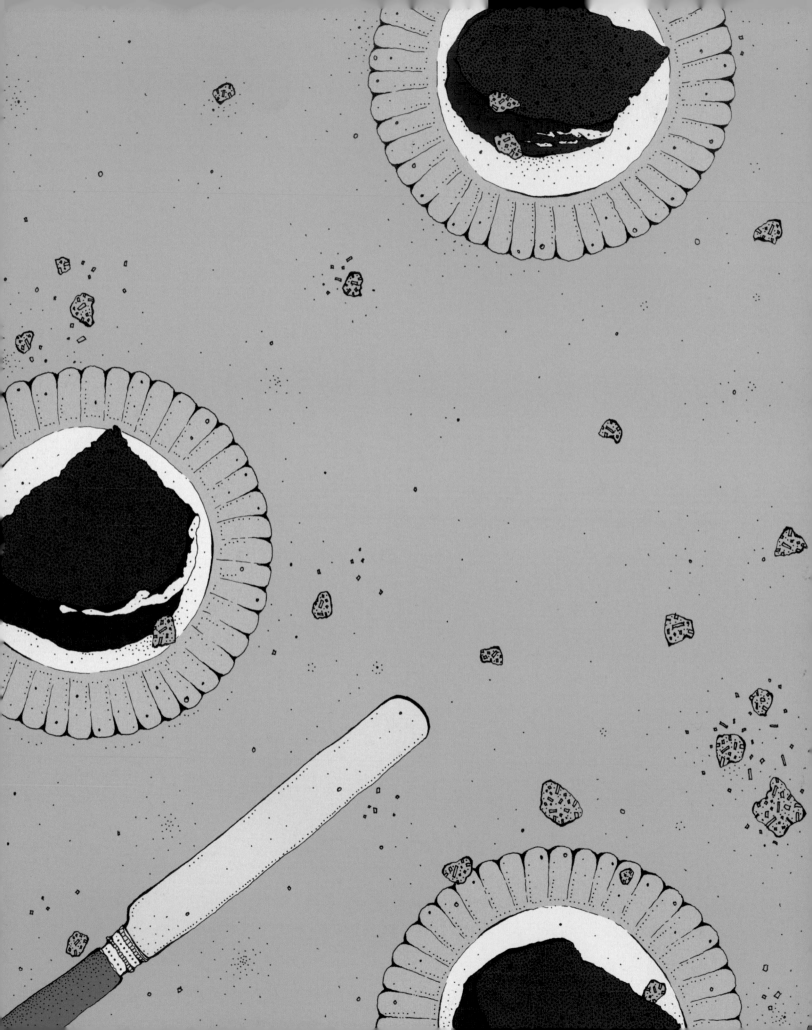

WHAT TO BAKE

&

HOW TO BAKE IT

What to Bake
& How to Bake It

For me, baking is many things: a loving gesture, a way to pitch in or show support or an invitation to a conversation. Sometimes it's just pure self-indulgence and the chance to step away from it all. I love baking because there's a recipe for every mood, occasion and person I know, a favourite flavour, ingredient or seasonal fruit. Baking is creative, scientific, a little bit magical and a lot of fun. And, of course, home-made always tastes better than shop-bought.

But what if you want to bake a birthday cake and don't know where to begin? Or you've been asked to cook for a bake sale last minute? Or feel stuck with just a few recipes that you've tried and trusted? Here's where this book comes in: a compilation of favourite family bakes, with something for every occasion and busy life, even if you've never baked before. If you're an experienced baker, there's plenty to discover and revisit. As a food writer and cookery teacher, I've been creating baking recipes for ten years now, but writing this book has taken me to new places – macarons, for instance, were something I usually bought rather than made. But now that I've worked out my way to make them simple, I'm hooked. And I've found ways to simplify and improve the most basic recipes, like Swiss roll or brownies, that I must have made 100 times before.

I've broken each recipe into several steps with all the detail a beginner needs. There's no substitute for actually being shown how to do something, so each step has a clear photo, and I've set out to make each recipe like a mini baking lesson; once you've cooked it, you'll want to bake it again, perhaps putting your own spin on it. New bakers will feel the confidence of a friendly voice behind each stir of the spoon.

The structure is designed with usefulness in mind too. The 50 recipes – mostly home-baking classics, with a few more adventurous ones – are grouped according to the occasion you might want to bake for. Simple Family Baking, which needs minimal bowls and time, is ideal for cooking with or for children; Morning Coffee & Afternoon Tea is a collection of easy-going bakes for any time of day; Special Bakes covers classics for Christmas and other times when you want to make a special effort; and Desserts & After Dinner offers recipes suited to finishing a meal. Many include helpful tips, offer ways to take a shortcut, use a different tin, make ahead or change flavours to suit you or the contents of the fridge better.

So many people tell me that they love cooking but can't bake. I don't take that challenge lightly and always hear myself repeating the baking mantra: have patience, measure carefully, read the recipe before you begin, and it will do what it's supposed to. What I do recommend, if you are new to baking, is that you take time to read the next few pages carefully, especially the part about measuring. Together, this careful approach of words and pictures really works; readers tell me in letters and emails that the first two books in the *What to Cook* series have turned them (or their partners, children, friends, neighbours) from complete beginners into confident cooks with a good basic repertoire. I hope that this book will do the same for would-be bakers. It will help you discover (or rediscover) the joy of baking at home, and experience that unbeatably proud feeling: 'I made that'.

Happy baking,

Jane Hornby

How to Make the Recipes Work For You

It's my job to take the guesswork out of baking for you, and each recipe contains all the information you need to know. However, if you are a new baker, reading this section will arm you with the whys and wherefores behind the recipes. Here are the most important tips for how to get the best out of them.

1

Measure carefully and get all the ingredients out before you begin.

2

Make sure ingredients are at the correct temperature, especially butter and eggs.

3

Don't make substitutions for ingredients or tins unless you absolutely have to.

4

Preheat the oven and grease and line any tins before you get started.

5

If a recipe contains bicarbonate of soda or baking powder, always mix them with the other dry ingredients first before sifting.

6

Try to get cakes into the oven as soon as possible once the batter has been mixed together.

7

Use a timer to keep track of your baking, and try not to peek or open the oven too much to avoid losing heat.

8

Let cakes and bakes settle for a while in the tin or on their baking tray before removing to a cooling rack.

Weighing & measuring

All the recipes in this book use metric grams (g) or millilitres (ml), plus teaspoon and tablespoon measures for smaller quantities. I prefer this method of measurement because it gives both flexibility for me when it comes to writing recipes, and accuracy for you when it comes to measuring. One cook's imperial ounce can often be quite different from another, but with grams there's no confusion. If you really do want to cook in pounds and ounces, stick to one method of measuring; don't combine metric and imperial in the same recipe, as this can lead to problems. Use a reliable conversion chart and follow it throughout.

A good set of scales is a must for baking. I recommend digital scales with a clear display, a tare function (which means you can reset it to zero and add another ingredient while the bowl is still on the scales), plus the ability to weigh in 5 g or smaller increments. You can measure liquids as well as dry goods using your scales, which is very handy, because 1 ml water, juice or milk weighs 1 g. I prefer to weigh thick liquids like yoghurt and buttermilk too, since it can be tricky to get an accurate level in a measuring jug. On that note, I'm quite pernickety about measuring spoons and jugs: make sure you buy a reputable brand for trustworthy results. It's best to use a small jug for smaller volumes of liquid, as the markings are not as precise on larger measuring jugs.

One standard tablespoon is 15 ml, one standard teaspoon is 5 ml, and there are 3 teaspoons in 1 tablespoon. In Australia, 1 tablespoon is 20 ml, or 4 teaspoons, so make adjustments as necessary. Unless stated otherwise, always fill the spoon to the top and level it off.

All eggs should be UK medium-sized eggs, which weigh about 60 g in their shells, and yield about 50 g once cracked. If you don't have the right egg size to hand, beat 1 more or 1 less egg, depending on the size you have, then measure the beaten amount, making sure you have 50 g for every egg used in the recipe.

For thick or sticky liquids such as treacle, I find it helpful to first very lightly oil the spoon I'm scooping from the jar with. This helps the liquid to flow from the spoon, giving the right quantity for the recipe.

Mastering Cakes

There are several methods for making cakes. The most common is the creaming method; a pound cake is a great example of a cake made this way. Some, like gingerbread, are melting-method cakes, which are dense and moist. Some use the muffin method, in which the wet ingredients are stirred into the dry ones. Less common are rubbed-together mixes like scones, and whisked cakes, such as the light sponge of a Swiss roll.

Creaming method
For this method, butter and sugar are beaten together thoroughly until pale and creamy looking, then eggs are added, followed by the other ingredients. You can do it by hand, but a stand mixer or hand-held electric beaters will give the best results. I find caster sugar is quicker and easier to cream than granulated. For perfect cakes, the butter needs to be soft enough to spoon easily, but not so warm that it's greasy or melted (see page 18). Add the room-temperature eggs gradually; if the batter looks curdled or lumpy when the eggs are going in (see page 18), add a little of the flour and it will become smooth again. Fold the flour and any liquid ingredients in carefully to preserve the air bubbles. Unless described otherwise, the batter should be 'soft dropping consistency' – which means that a spoonful of batter should be soft enough to drop easily into the bowl when given a gentle shake.

I've made some of my creaming-method cakes using a speedier all-in-one method, in which the butter and sugar are first creamed, then everything else goes in the bowl at once and is beaten briefly to make a smooth batter. To take this shortcut yourself in other creamed recipes, add 1 extra teaspoon baking powder to the dry ingredients, then follow as above.

Melting & muffin methods

Melting-method cakes are great for beginners, as the fat and sugar are simply melted together. Make sure they have cooled before adding the rest of the ingredients. These cakes tend to keep well. The muffin method simply involves mixing all the wet ingredients into the dry ones. To keep your cake light, try not to overmix or overbake it.

Rubbing-in method

This is a way of combining fat with flour, either by hand or in a processor, until they look like fine breadcrumbs, then liquid is added to make a dough. The butter must be cold and the dough must not be overmixed.

Whisking method

Whisked cakes can be the trickiest, and rely on the air beaten into the eggs to make them rise, rather than on raising agents like baking powder. Make sure the eggs are at room temperature and beat them with the sugar until very pale and thick. Fold in the dry ingredients very carefully to preserve the air.

Meringues

When making meringues, make sure the bowl and beaters are spotlessly clean. The term 'stiff peaks' means that the beaten egg whites will hold their shape. Pull the beaters away from the bowl and hold them upright. If the whites fall or flop, they're not ready. If they point upwards or hold a stiff curve, they're ready. Don't add the sugar until this point, and be careful not to overwhisk them (see page 19). A meringue batter at stiff-peak stage with sugar added will be very thick and pearly, like shaving foam.

Tin sizes

For predictable baking, choose the correct size of tin for the recipe whenever you can. If you do have to substitute, remember that square tins have larger volumes than round ones, so use a square tin that's 2.5 cm smaller than its round equivalent, and vice versa. Check that your tin is about the same volume as the tin specified in the recipe: a standard 20-cm round (4.5 cm deep) sandwich tin holds about 1 litre; a deeper 23-cm round springform tin holds about 2.5 litres; a 25-cm bundt tin holds 2.8 litres; a 23 x 33-cm traybake or roasting tin holds 3.8 litres; a 23-cm shallow square traybake tin holds 1.7 litres; and a 23 x 12-cm (or 2-lb) loaf tin with sloping sides, 1 litre. If you're unsure, use a smaller tin and discard some of the batter rather than using one that's too large. Never fill a tin more than two-thirds full, and check carefully that the cake is ready, as baking times may vary slightly.

Is it ready?

There are varying stages of readiness, depending on the recipe. Most cakes can be tested with a skewer, a cocktail stick or, if you're really stuck, a strand of spaghetti. Insert it into the centre; when you pull it out, a cooked cake will leave no trace, apart from a few damp crumbs or a little oiliness. If you see raw batter, it needs to go back into the oven as soon as possible. Test again in 5–10 minutes. If it wobbles or looks wet in the middle, don't test it yet; close the oven door carefully and check in 10–15 minutes. Some cakes can look cooked on the outside, but are still wet in the middle. In that case, cover it with a loose 'hat' of foil, then continue to cook. The cake will not burn on the top before the centre is done.

Other cues that tell you it's ready: the cake has risen all the way across the middle, possibly with cracks that look dry at the bottom. The sides will have shrunk away slightly from the tin and the cake will have an even golden colour. Some things that we want to be gooey in the middle (like brownies) will jiggle instead. The surface should look set, but as you gently shake the tin you'll see a slight wobble under the surface. It won't look like there's liquid under there, but rather a set jelly.

Turning it out & letting it cool

Most cakes benefit from being left to cool in the tin for 10–15 minutes before being transferred to a cooling rack. To remove a cake from a tin with a removable base, sit the tin on something narrow and tall, such as a jam jar. Press the tin down onto the jar and the sides will slide down. Use a palette knife to loosen between the lining paper and the tin. If the tin does not have removable sides or base, put something flat, like a plate or board, over it, then flip the tin upside down. Remove the tin, loosen the lining paper, then flip the cake onto a cooling rack. Take care if the top of the cake is delicate. Lift traybakes out by their lining paper; if the cake starts to sag a bit as you lift, get a helper to lift one side while you lift the other.

Perfect frosting

Making frosting is easy, but practice makes perfect when it comes to covering a cake like a pro; see the recipes on page 134 and 160 for advice. Bear in mind that icings and glazes often need to be thicker than you think, so measure liquid ingredients carefully and add more icing sugar if needed to thicken it up. Most cakes need to be completely cold before frosting or icing.

Cutting & serving

For sponge cakes, use a long, sharp serrated knife with a pointy end. Use a sharp non-serrated knife for firmer cakes like cheesecake and brownies. If your cake is frosted, wipe the knife on kitchen paper before each cut. If splitting a cake in half to create layers, chilling it first makes a neater job. The key to cutting a large cake to serve a lot of people is to do it in a grid. Cut across the cake to give rectangular 2.5 x 5-cm slices (the offcuts are the chef's perk).

Storing & freezing cakes

To store baked goods in the cupboard, you can't beat an old-fashioned airtight metal cake tin. Always store them in a cool place, but only in the fridge if specified. If you want to get ahead, freezing cakes before frosting them (rather than storing them at room temperature) will keep them fresher, even for just a few days. Use sealable large freezer bags and plastic boxes and remove as much air as you can. Most will be fine in the freezer for up to 1 month. Defrost overnight, then frost or glaze. Most bakes have the best flavour and texture when eaten at, or near, room temperature. If your cake is chilled, make sure you remove it from the fridge in good time.

What went wrong?

I hope none of the following things happens to your cakes, but there's always a reason for a cake not working properly, so you can fix it next time.

FLAT CAKE
Left too long before going into the oven. Inadequate whisking or heavy-handed folding. Oven too low. Old baking powder or bicarbonate of soda.

OVERFLOWING CAKE
Tin too small, too much raising agent, too much liquid or not enough flour due to incorrect measuring.

SUNKEN CAKE
Removed from the oven too soon.

DRY OR OVERCOOKED CAKE
Oven too hot or baked for too long. Cake batter not 'soft dropping consistency' (see page 85), if the recipe states it should have been.

CRACKED CAKE
Personally, I love some cakes with cracks in them, and I often design a recipe to have one on purpose! If your cake ends up cracked when you don't want it to be, it's normally due to the oven being too hot or the tin too small.

BIG BUBBLES OR HOLES
Insufficient mixing and sifting of raising agents into the flour. Batter left too long before going into the oven.

Mastering Pastry, Cookies & Bread

Pastry

There are three kinds of pastry in this book: sweet shortcrust, used for pies; choux paste, for profiteroles; and a richer sweet pastry, which is perfect for delicate tarts and some cookies. You can of course buy ready-made dough and pastry cases, but making most pastry is simple and quick, especially if you have a food processor. In general, crisp yet tender shortcrust pastry needs cold fat and little handling for the best results. The fat and flour are rubbed together until they look like fine breadcrumbs. Very little liquid is then added to bring the dough together. It should feel dry to the touch, but should not crack or crumble. If you do need to add more liquid, add 1 teaspoon at a time and try not to overwork the dough as you add it. Shortcrust pastry and the rich pastry mentioned above should be kept cool and rested before rolling it out. This helps prevent shrinking later and makes them easier to roll. If the dough starts being tricky to work with, chill it and try again.

Blind baking

This simply means baking the pastry twice before filling it, to avoid any sogginess or shrinkage. For the first bake, the cold pastry is lined with foil and held in place with baking beans (see page 14). These conduct the heat from the oven to the pastry, and help it to set in position. Without the foil and beans, the pastry would slip down the sides of the tin or bubble. The pastry is then baked again until cooked through. Pastry is dry and feels sandy when it's ready, and doesn't always need to be dark golden before it's done; it depends on the recipe. Shortcrust pastry is very fragile when hot, and should be cooled in the tin. If you want to serve a tart or pie warm, just take it to the table in the tin.

Cookies

When making cookies and biscuits, try not to overwork the dough once the flour has been added, as this can make them tough. Measure raising agents accurately and leave plenty of room for them to spread on the baking trays. They can burn easily so keep an eye on the cooking time. Always leave them to cool on a cooling rack before transferring to an airtight container.

Bread doughs

When strong bread flour and liquid are kneaded together, strands of gluten form, which give bread its structure. Kneading it well (see page 69) is important to help the gluten develop. Don't be afraid of a wet or sticky dough; it will give you a better loaf. I use fast-action yeast for no-fuss baking, which can be added straight to the flour. Make sure your yeast is within the use-by date, and the liquid is not too hot. Find a warm, not draughty, place to let your dough rise, and cover it with oiled clingfilm or a tea towel to prevent a skin forming. Once doubled in size, shape the bread (if it gets too springy, let it rest for 5 minutes) then leave to prove, which means to rise for a second, shorter time. To check the proving, gently press the side of the dough. If it doesn't spring back, it's ready to bake. Once baked, the base will be firm and sound hollow when tapped.

Freezing & storing other baked goods

Pastry, cookies and bread are also ideal for the freezer and can be stored in the same way as cakes. Raw pastry can be chilled for 1 week or frozen for 1 month (shaped in its tin, if you like). Freeze small items flat on a baking tray, then pack them into bags or boxes, layers interleaved with baking parchment and all air squeezed out. Refresh cooked bread and choux pastry in a hot oven for a few minutes. Store cooked pastry and cookies in airtight containers.

Equipment

Most of the recipes here are achievable by hand or machine, depending on your preference, and what equipment you are likely to have. Machines will certainly make many of them easier. See pages 14–17 for photographs.

Hand-held electric mixers

I find these invaluable for baking, although most things can also be done with a good old wooden spoon or whisk. Hand-held electric mixers save time, do a great job and are more affordable than stand mixers.

Food processors & stand mixers

If you have a stand mixer, use it whenever you prefer for beating, whipping and kneading. Food processors are great for making pastry, as they help work the dough together more quickly and use less liquid. They're also good for kneading dough using the plastic dough blade. Prep work, such as chopping nuts, is made faster, and rubbing in is transformed into a 1-minute job.

Ovens

There are three main kinds of oven: conventional electric, fan (or convection) electric and gas. Conventional ovens emit heat from the top and bottom, fan ovens blow heat from the back, and gas ovens tend to heat from the bottom only. I have given the temperatures for cooking in all three kinds of oven, and you'll notice that the fan cooking temperature is 20 degrees lower than the conventional. This is because fan ovens cook more quickly (and as a bonus, more evenly), due to the effect of the circulating hot air. This is standard practice, but check in your oven manual if you still have it, and adjust as needed.

Oven thermostats are only accurate to a point, which is why it's best to be aware of what you are looking for as well as how long the recipe says it should cook for. Use a timer, plus the other sensory cues described on page 9 and 11, and in the recipe, to decide if it's ready. Sometimes you'll need to turn a tin around as it cooks, especially if baking two things at once. Be quick, taking care not to let too much hot air out or cold air in. Get to know your oven: sometimes the top or bottom shelves are hotter than the middle ones. Bake bread and pastry in the hottest part, and cakes and cookies in the middle.

Tins

Heavy, good-quality tins are best, and ideally with a pale finish. Darker tins can cause cakes and other bakes to brown too much, and sometimes shorten cooking times a little. Most of the tins called for here are non-stick.

Preparing tins

Lining a tin is useful for two reasons: It helps you get the cake out of the tin and also acts as a layer of insulation, protecting the edges from overcooking. I mainly use butter to grease the tin before lining; just add enough to get the paper to stick. Non-stick vegetable oil spray is a quick alternative if you are short of time. Baking parchment is non-stick with a silicone coating, and is ideal for most recipes. If you only have greaseproof paper, grease the paper as well as the tin. Re-usable silicone mats are a good choice and can be cut to size. Scones and breads can be baked using a little flour underneath instead. Muffins and cupcakes can go into their own paper cases or a greased non-stick tin.

Ingredients

Flour

Try to use good-quality flour, as this is the foundation of most of your baking. I've used plain flour and added my own raising agents (baking powder or bicarbonate of soda or both) instead of using self-raising flour, because this lets me control exactly how much each cake rises. Some of the cake recipes include cornflour, which lowers the overall protein content of the flour and gives a particularly tender cake. Bread, however, needs strong bread flour, with a high protein content that gives plenty of structure to the dough. Flours can vary a little in water content, which is why some doughs and batters may seem dry, even if you have followed the recipe exactly; you can always add a splash more liquid.

Gluten-free baking

If you prefer to substitute gluten-free flour for wheat flour, use a reputable brand and follow the instructions. You may also find xanthan gum useful.

Sugars & sweeteners

Caster sugar is ideal for most baking, as it creams very effectively with butter for fluffy cakes, and dissolves quickly into batters and doughs. However, when a type of sugar is not specified, you can use caster or granulated. 'Golden' unrefined versions will work perfectly well too, but give your bakes a slightly darker colour. Avoid substituting honey or maple syrup for either sugar or golden syrup, as this will cause the recipe to behave differently.

Butter & oils

Unsalted butter is best for baking, and I don't recommend substituting margarine, which can really alter the balance of a recipe. Butter must be the right temperature, usually soft and room temperature for cakes, but cold for pastry. Choose a flavourless oil for baking, such as sunflower, unless stated otherwise.

Dairy products

Choose full-fat yoghurt, cream cheeses and whole milk for the recipes in this book. Double cream is the best all-round choice for cooking, as it can be poured, whipped and boiled. Full-fat crème fraîche makes a good alternative to double cream in most cases, and can be whipped to fill cakes or heated for frostings and sauces. Do not try to boil single, soured or reduced-fat cream, as it will split. Buttermilk makes lovely cakes and scones, and is easily substituted if you can't find it (see page 31). Use dairy products straight from the fridge.

Eggs

Use fresh, free-range, good-quality UK medium-sized eggs. If you have older eggs to use up, they will create good meringues and are great for whisked cakes as they can whip up to a greater volume. Use eggs at the right temperature: room temperature for creamed-method and whisking cakes, cold for pastry.

Chocolate

For me, the best day-to-day chocolate for baking has 60% cocoa solids, which has a good, deep flavour but is easier to work with than the intensely chocolatey 70% cocoa variety. Unfortunately it's harder to find. So, to make 60% chocolate, I just melt equal quantities of 50% and 70% chocolates (see page 57). Take care when melting chocolate; follow the instructions in the recipes carefully.

Citrus fruit

When using citrus fruits for zesting, use unwaxed fruit, or scrub well in soapy water before you start grating.

Baking Trays & Tins

1
23-cm fluted tart tin: a tin with a removable base for tarts and pies with a delicate look, 3–4 cm deep.

2
Wire cooling rack: a large, non-stick one is good; if you plan to bake a lot, you'll find it useful to have two.

3
Flat baking tray: this has a lip on one side to hold on to, but the other edges are flat, making it easy to slide things on and off.

4
23-cm round springform cake tin: for cheesecakes, large dessert cakes that look elegant when cut into long, shallow slices and large celebration cakes.

5
Baking beans: ceramic balls that are essential for blind baking. You can also use dried pulses or rice, although they don't have such good heat-conducting properties.

6
23-cm pie tin: for classic deep-dish pies. Choose a metal one with a rim, as this will give you something for a crimped edge to stick to, and means you can add a lid, if you like.

7
20-cm round loose-based 'sandwich' tins: ideal for layer cakes that are quick to bake. About 4.5 cm deep is best, which will make cakes deep enough for cutting in half horizontally.

8
Deep 20-cm round cake tin: ideal for Christmas cakes and other fruit cakes.

14

1–3

4

5–6

7

8

1
Muffin tin and muffin cases
with deep wells.

2
Bundt tin: creates a wonderfully
shaped cake. The central chimney
delivers heat to the centre of the
cake, which speeds up cooking
and gives a very tender result.
Normally 25 cm.

3
23-cm square brownie tin: perfect
for all sorts of bars and sliceable
baked goods.

4
Standard '2-lb' loaf tin: measures
23 x 12 cm along the top inside
edges. I prefer one with sloping
sides, as straight edges mean the
tin is larger and cakes don't rise into
such a nice shape.

5
23 x 33-cm traybake (or roasting)
tin: perfect for simple large bakes
that can be cut into squares or
carved into a novelty shape.

6
25 x 37-cm Swiss roll tin: wide
enough to use as a baking tray too.

7
Angel food cake tin: 25 cm, straight-
sided and deep, this is probably the
only tin that cannot be substituted.

Utensils & Equipment

1
Food processor: for chopping and quick prep. This one has a 20-cm diameter bowl, 12 cm deep, which is big enough to make cakes.

2
Mixing bowls of various sizes: you'll need at least one large bowl that is big enough to beat in and splash batter without it spilling over the edges. Pyrex bowls are ideal as they are heat resistant, can go in the microwave and also stack neatly.

3
Large metal spoon for folding: the larger the spoon, the less folding you'll have to do, and the finer the metal, the more sharply it cuts through the batter.

4
Sieves: choose one with a medium mesh for the large sieve, as it can be frustratingly slow sifting flour through a fine-mesh sieve. Make the mini sieve a fine one, for dusting sugar over finished recipes.

5
Rubber spatula: It should be flexible to help you scrape out the bowl, and a thin edge is good for folding.

6
Wooden spoon

7
Whisk: metal is a more durable choice than plastic, although it can scratch some pans.

8
Hand-held electric mixer: this is very handy, but you can also use a stand mixer.

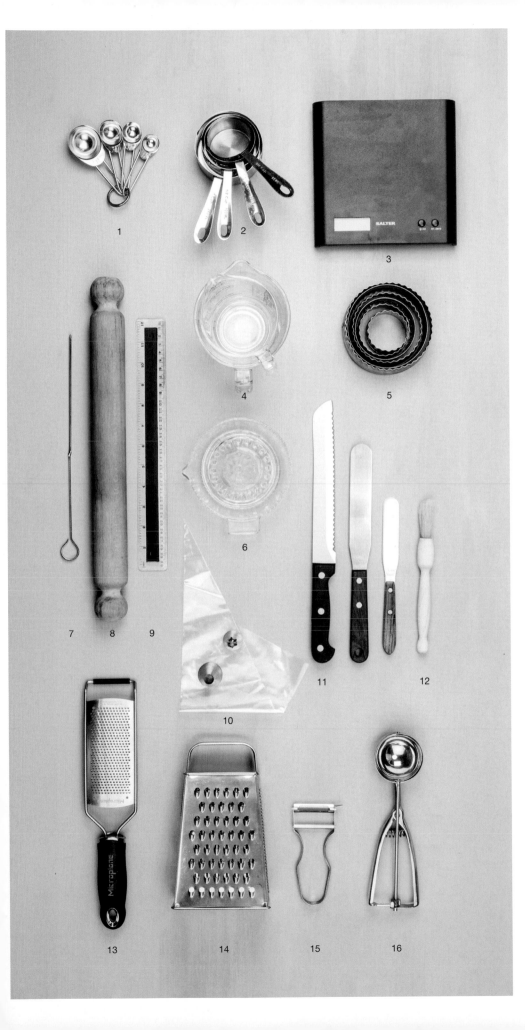

1
Measuring spoons: 1 tablespoon, and ¼, ½ and 1 teaspoon.

2
Measuring cups: standard British and Australian cups hold 250 ml.

3
Kitchen scales

4
Measuring jugs

5
Pastry cutters

6
Citrus fruit juicer

7
Skewer

8
Rolling pin: the straight part should be at least 30 cm long. Avoid those with a central spindle.

9
Ruler

10
Piping bag and nozzles: disposable bags are simple to use.

11
Bread knife or long serrated knife, plus small and large palette knives.

12
Pastry brush

13
Fine grater

14
Box grater

15
Peeler

16
Large ice-cream scoop

What to Look For

1

Softened butter: The butter should be soft but not greasy, so that it can easily be spooned or beaten in a large bowl. If it seems too hard, warm it for just a couple of seconds in the microwave at medium power. Alternatively, cut it into small pieces and set it aside in a warm place. If it's too soft, put the bowl in the fridge or freezer for a few minutes and try again.

2

Creaming: The bowl on the left shows butter and sugar that have been beaten together, but not to the right extent.

The bowl on the right shows the correct creamy, very pale mixture, which has increased quite a bit in volume and changed from yellow to almost white.

3

Split batter: The bowl on the left shows creamed butter and sugar to which the egg has been added rather too quickly. The mixture has split and looks lumpy or slimy. This is the point at which you will need to add 1 tablespoon flour; adding more egg will make things worse, and a split batter can lead to a poor rise.

The bowl on the right has not split, and is light and fluffy.

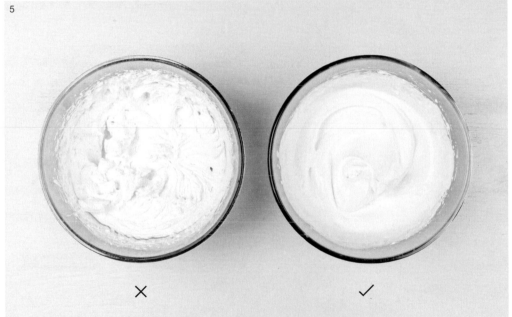

4

Overwhisked egg whites: The bowl on the left shows egg whites before adding any sugar, which have been overbeaten. They look dry and have started to break up at the edges. There's not much of a fix for this, so take care while you whisk.

The bowl on the right shows the time to stop whisking and start adding sugar to make meringues; it is thick and stiff, but not dry.

5

Whipped cream: The bowl on the left shows cream that has been overwhipped and is turning thick and lumpy. This won't spread well and can be very hard to fold into other ingredients.

The bowl on the right shows perfectly whipped cream, soft and thickened. Cream thickens while it stands and as you pipe or spread it, so it's always best to under-whip it.

6

Overcooked chocolate: This shows burnt chocolate, which has turned thick and granular. Take care to melt chocolate carefully, as once it's like this, it can't be used.

SIMPLE
FAMILY BAKING

Golden Citrus Drizzle Cake

Preparation time: 15 minutes
Baking time: 35 minutes
Makes 12 large squares,
or more fingers

In my experience, a citrus drizzle
cake always disappears first from the
table at a fête or bake sale, so I've
re-created it as a traybake that's
easy to make, slice and transport.
Cornmeal or polenta adds a golden
glow to the inside, but if you prefer
you can substitute the same amount
of plain flour.

For the cake

225 g soft butter, plus extra
    for greasing
2 lemons
2 limes
1 tangerine, mandarin or clementine,
    with a vibrant orange skin
200 g caster sugar
4 eggs, room temperature
125 g plain flour
125 g fine yellow cornmeal
    or quick-cook polenta
¼ tsp salt
2 tsp baking powder
125 g lemon-flavoured or plain
    whole yoghurt

For the topping

100 g caster sugar, or granulated for
    extra crunch

1
Preheat the oven to 180°C (160°C fan/gas 4). Grease a 23-cm shallow square tin with butter, then line it with baking parchment. Finely grate the zest from all the fruit, taking care not to remove the bitter white pith just underneath the colourful outer layer. Put 2 teaspoons of the mixed zests in a large bowl with the butter and sugar, saving the rest for later.

LOVE LEMONS? LIME-AHOLIC?
For a straight-up lemon cake or lime cake, simply use the zest and juice from one kind of fruit (you'll need 4 teaspoons zest and 80 ml juice). I find all orange a little too sweet for a drizzle cake, so add a little lemon juice and zest for extra bite.

2
Using an electric mixer, beat the butter and sugar together until creamy and pale. Scrape the sides of the bowl down every now and again with a spatula, so that every last bit gets mixed.

3
Crack the eggs into a measuring jug (I do this because they plop from it individually, which is easier than stopping the beaters to crack an egg every now and again). Pour one egg into the bowl, then beat it into the creamed mixture until completely combined, fluffy and light. Add the rest of the eggs one by one, beating well each time. If the mixture starts to look at all slimy, add 1 tablespoon of the flour and it will become smooth again.

MAKE IT BIGGER
To make a traybake, grease and line a 23 x 33-cm traybake tin and double the quantities. Bake at 180°C (160°C fan/gas 4) for 25 minutes, then at 160°C (140°C fan/gas 3) for 25 minutes, or until a skewer comes out clean. Double the drizzle quantities too.

4

Thoroughly mix together the flour, cornmeal or polenta, salt and baking powder, then sift half of it on top of the egg mixture. Using a spatula or a large metal spoon, fold it in until the batter is thick and fairly smooth.

5

Fold in the yoghurt in the same way, then sift over and fold in the remaining dry ingredients. Scrape the batter into the prepared tin, level the top, then give it a sharp tap on the work surface to help remove any bubbles that can sometimes appear in this cake. Bake for 20 minutes, or until it is golden and has risen all over, then turn the oven down to 160°C (140°C fan/gas 3). If it's browning too much on one side, quickly and carefully turn it around. Bake for another 15 minutes, or until firm to the touch, or it passes the skewer test (see page 32). Leave to cool in the tin on a wire rack for a few minutes.

6

Meanwhile, squeeze the juice from 1 lemon, 1 lime and half the tangerine, to make about 80 ml. Poke 20 or so holes all over the cake using a fine skewer or a cocktail stick. Mix the sugar for the topping into the juice (do not let it dissolve), then spoon it over the surface of the still-warm cake, making sure that the sugar looks thick and evenly spread.

7

Leave to cool completely. The sugar will become crisp and sparkly once the syrup soaks into the cake. Cut into squares to serve. If making the cake a day ahead, leave it loosely covered or in a roomy container with a little air for breathing. This will keep the sugary crust crisp.

Fruity Cupcakes

Preparation time: 10 minutes
Baking time: 18–20 minutes
Makes 12 ordinary or 24 fairy cakes

All kids love to make cupcakes, right? But the eating (for this grownup, anyway) doesn't always quite live up to the excitement, so that's why this recipe is generous with the milk to make a fluffy cake with no hint of dryness about it. The fruit glaze is easily swapped for one of the other quick frostings in the book, if you prefer.

For the cakes

110 g soft butter

150 g caster sugar

185 g plain flour

1 tbsp cornflour

1½ tsp baking powder

¼ tsp salt

2 eggs, room temperature

½ tsp vanilla extract or paste

120 ml milk

For the fruity glaze

about 65 g berries (fresh or frozen and defrosted) or 2 large, ripe passion fruit

125–150 g icing sugar

1
Preheat the oven to 180°C (160°C fan/gas 4). Line a 12-hole muffin tin with deep paper cases. Beat the butter and sugar together until pale and creamy. You can do this with a hand-held electric mixer, but a wooden spoon is fine if you are cooking with children.

2
In another smaller bowl, mix together the flour, cornflour, baking powder and salt, then sift half of this mixture on top of the creamed butter and sugar. Add the eggs, vanilla and half the milk too.

3
Beat the ingredients together, starting slowly at first, and keep going until creamy and smooth. In separate additions, add the rest of the flour mixture and then the milk, beating after each, to make a very soft batter. Don't worry if it looks a little separated once all the milk is in. Spoon the batter into the prepared tin, aiming for an equal amount in each paper case.

MAKING SMALLER CAKES
If you prefer, this batter will also make 24 smaller fairy cakes baked in shallow bun tins lined with fairy cake cases. Bake for 15 minutes, or until golden and risen.

4

Bake for 18–20 minutes, or until the cakes have risen and are golden, and a skewer inserted into one of the central cakes comes out clean. If they start to brown unevenly during cooking, turn the tin around in the oven and continue to bake. Cool in the tin for 5 minutes, then transfer to a rack.

5

To make a berry glaze, use the back of a fork to crush the berries until juicy and well mashed. Sift the icing sugar into the bowl, then stir to combine. For a passion fruit glaze, scoop the seeds and pulp from the fruit (you'll need about 4 tablespoons) and mix with the sifted icing sugar. If either icing seems too runny, add a little more sugar (it will depend on the individual fruits and how juicy they are). Spoon the glaze over the cooled cakes and leave to set.

6

The cakes are best enjoyed as soon as the glaze has set, or can be kept in an airtight container for a couple of days. Un-iced cakes can be frozen for up to 1 month, then decorated once defrosted.

BUTTERFLY CAKES
To make this teatime classic, use a small serrated knife to cut the tops off the cakes, then cut each top in half to make two semi-circles. Make the buttercream frosting on page 46. Spoon a generous dollop of buttercream on top of each of the cakes, then poke the 'wings' into the cream at an angle, golden-side up, with the curved edges facing away from each other. Add a little dot of jam, lemon curd or some sprinkles, and dust with icing sugar to serve. You could also use sweetened whipped cream.

Buttermilk Pound Cake

Preparation time: 15 minutes
Baking time: 50–55 minutes
Cuts into 8–10 slices

Pound cake isn't fancy or smart, but has a reliable, rustic beauty. Served just as it is, or as a dessert with soft fruit and a dollop of cream, or perhaps covered with thick, lemony icing dripping down the sides for coffee time, this cake seems to fit any occasion. For flavour variations, turn to page 32.

175 g soft butter, plus extra
   for greasing
175 g caster sugar
3 eggs, room temperature
1 tsp vanilla extract
225 g plain flour
½ tsp bicarbonate of soda
½ tsp baking powder
¼ tsp salt
120 g buttermilk (or see Tip)
1 tbsp icing sugar
   (optional)

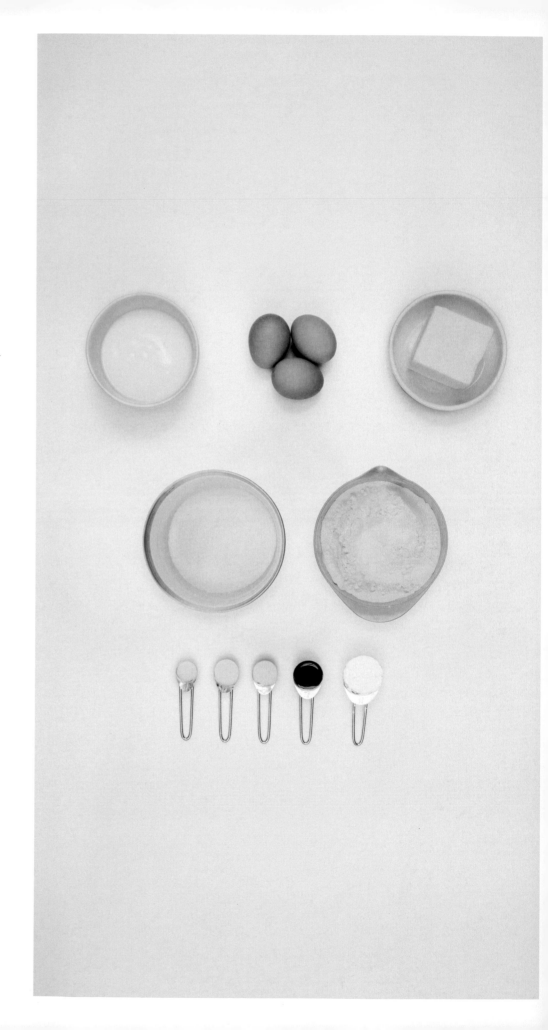

1

Grease a 23 x 12-cm loaf tin with a little butter, then line it with baking parchment. Cut a long, thin strip for the length of the tin, then another to go across the width, leaving some overhang on each side to make it easy to lift out the cake later. Preheat the oven to 180°C (160°C fan/gas 4). Using an electric mixer, beat the butter and sugar together until very creamy and pale. Scrape the sides of the bowl down every now and again with a spatula, so that every last bit gets mixed.

2

Crack the eggs into a measuring jug and beat well with a fork. Pour about 2 tablespoons egg into the butter mixture, then beat until the egg is incorporated and the mixture becomes light and fluffy. Repeat, adding a little egg at a time, until all of the egg has been worked in. If the mixture starts to look at all slimy or lumpy, add 1 tablespoon of the flour and it will become smooth again. Beat in the vanilla.

3

Stir together the flour, bicarbonate of soda, baking powder and salt. Sift half of it on top of the beaten egg mixture, then fold in with a large metal spoon or spatula. Fold in the buttermilk, then repeat with remaining flour mixture to make a smooth, thick batter.

NO BUTTERMILK?
This cake can be made with milk instead. Measure 120 ml milk, then replace 2 tablespoons of it with lemon juice. Leave to stand for a few minutes until thickened, then use as above.

4

Scrape the batter into the tin, then gently level the top.

5

Bake for 30 minutes, or until it has risen and cracked in the centre, then turn the oven down to 160°C (140°C fan/gas 3) and bake for 20–25 minutes more, until a skewer comes out clean. Leave to cool in the tin for 15 minutes, then remove from the tin using the lining paper to help. Leave to cool on a wire rack.

THE SKEWER TEST
When any kind of sponge cake is ready, a skewer or cocktail stick inserted into the centre will come out clean (possibly a little greasy-looking), or with a few damp crumbs attached. If it has raw cake batter on the end, the cake is not ready and should be baked for 5–10 minutes longer before testing again.

6

Once cooled, peel off the baking parchment. Sift the icing sugar over the top, or try one of the ideas below. This is at its best on the day of baking, but will keep in an airtight container, or can be frozen (without icing, if using) for up to 1 month.

LEMON CAKE
Add the zest of 1 lemon and only ½ teaspoon vanilla extract in step 2. Stir 3½ teaspoons lemon juice into 100 g sifted icing sugar until smooth, spoon it all over the cooled cake, then leave to set.

STICKY MARMALADE CAKE
Use orange zest in the batter. Warm 4 tablespoons marmalade with 1 tablespoon citrus juice or water and brush it over the warm cake.

CLASSIC SEED CAKE
Toast 1 teaspoon caraway seeds in a hot dry pan to release the aroma. Fold them in and bake as before.

Peanut Butter Cookies

Preparation time: 15 minutes
Baking time: 10–12 minutes per batch
Makes 24

These have everything I look for in a peanut butter cookie: a slightly soft inside, a crisp outside and a salty sweetness that means one is never enough. Like most home-made cookies, they are best eaten on the day of baking – no real hardship there! There's a make-ahead option if you prefer; see over the page.

---

140 g whole unsalted roasted
 peanuts
250 g plain flour
½ tsp baking powder
80 g light brown soft sugar
80 g caster sugar
½ tsp salt
140 g butter, room temperature
100 g smooth peanut butter
1 egg
2 tbsp clear honey

1

Preheat the oven to 180°C (160°C fan/gas 4). Spread the nuts over a baking tray and cook for about 8 minutes, or until pale golden. This step isn't essential if you're in a hurry, but it adds an extra deep, nutty flavour.

CAN'T FIND UNSALTED PEANUTS? You could also use salted roasted nuts (the snacking kind) for this recipe. Skip straight to step 2 and add only a pinch of salt to the dough instead of ½ teaspoon.

2

Chop the nuts with a knife, or use a food processor. I prefer mine quite chunky, but go as fine as you like.

3

Put the flour, baking powder, sugars and salt in a large bowl and mix together. Cut the butter into cubes and add it to the bowl with the peanut butter.

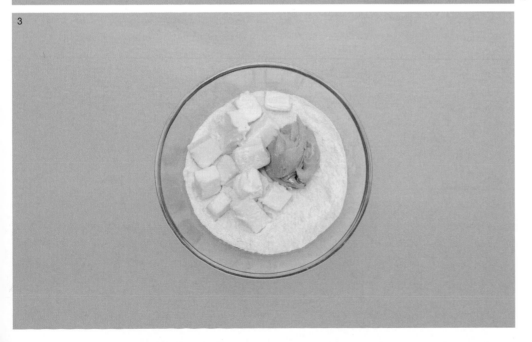

4

Rub the peanut butter and butter into the dry ingredients using your fingers and thumbs. To do this, use both hands to lift some of the butter, peanut butter and flour from the bowl. Gently pinch the butters and flour together as they pass through your fingers back into the bowl. Keep going, and eventually you will have a mixture that looks like fine crumbs. You can do this with a food processor, if you prefer. Beat the egg. Add two thirds of the chopped toasted peanuts to the mixture, then the egg and honey.

5

Mix everything together with a table knife or wooden spoon to make a rough, fairly sticky dough. Try not to overwork it, as this can make your cookies tough.

MAKE AHEAD
You can shape the dough into 2 logs about 7.5 cm across, roll each one in the nuts (chopped a little finer), then wrap tightly in clingfilm and chill or freeze. Slice and bake the cookies as you need them.

6

Line 2 flat baking trays with baking parchment. Pinch off a walnut-sized ball of dough and roll it between your palms until smooth. Press the ball into the remaining chopped nuts, squishing it to a flatter disc. Place nut-side up on the baking tray, then repeat. Leave plenty of space between the cookies.

7

Bake for 10–12 minutes (about 13 minutes from frozen), or until evenly golden. Roll and squash the next batch of cookies while the first batch bakes. Leave them to cool on the baking trays for a few minutes before transferring to a rack to cool completely. Store in an airtight container and eat within 3 days.

Favourite Swiss Roll

Preparation time: 15 minutes
Baking time: 10 minutes
Makes 10 slices

A Swiss roll was one of the first
things I ever baked with my mum,
probably because it was so quick
to make, and all the ingredients were
in the cupboard. Although there
are lots of steps, be assured that it's
a simple cake, and one of the most
popular among friends and family
when I was creating the recipes for
this book.

For the cake

50 g butter, plus extra for greasing

3 tbsp milk

4 eggs, room temperature

150 g caster sugar

1 tbsp cornflour

125 g plain flour

¼ tsp salt

For rolling and filling

4 tbsp caster sugar

250 g raspberry jam or jelly

1
Use plenty of butter to grease the base and sides of a 25 x 37-cm (or thereabouts) Swiss roll tin or rimmed baking tray, then line the base with baking parchment. Preheat the oven to 200°C (180°C fan/gas 6). Put the milk and butter in a small pan and heat gently until the butter melts. Set aside (it will need to be warm when you use it).

2
Put the eggs and the sugar in a large bowl and whisk with an electric mixer at medium speed until thick, moussey and doubled in volume – about 5 minutes.

3
Stir the cornflour, flour and salt together, then sift them on top of the eggs. Fold together well using a large metal spoon or spatula, cutting and lifting the flour through the foam instead of stirring it. This will preserve the air bubbles and ensure a light and fluffy cake.

4
Pour the warm butter and milk around the edge of the batter bowl. Using the large spoon or spatula, fold until evenly combined. The liquid can pool at the bottom of the bowl, so be persistent, trying not to knock out too much air.

5
Carefully pour the batter into the prepared tin, then tilt it slowly from side to side, letting the batter run into the corners. If it still looks uneven, spread out the batter very gently with a spatula. Don't worry if you see a little dry flour or ribbons of butter – just work them in gently. The batter will completely fill the tin, but don't worry, it won't spill over as it bakes.

6

Bake for 10 minutes, or until the cake is golden, has risen and the edges have shrunk away from the sides of the tin. Meanwhile, dust a larger sheet of baking parchment with 2 tablespoons sugar. Loosen the edges of the cake with a palette knife, then sprinkle the remaining sugar on top.

7

Swiftly flip the cake onto the sugared baking parchment. Carefully peel off the paper that lined the tin. Using a serrated knife, trim about 1 cm off from each edge. Score a line into the cake about 2.5 cm in from the short end nearest you. This will make it easier to roll.

8

While the cake is still hot, roll it up from the short end, rolling the sugared paper inside the cake. Don't rush things, and if a few cracks appear, don't worry.

9

Cover the cake in a clean tea towel and leave to cool until just warm.

10

Unwrap and unroll the cake, then spread it with the jam. Roll the cake up again, using one hand to guide it and the other to pull the sugared paper underneath it upwards. This will help keep the spiral fairly tight.

FILLING WITH CREAM?
To fill with whipped cream (see page 48) or buttercream (see page 46), the cake must be cold. Whipped cream can go straight on top of the jam. For buttercream, spread it out first, then cover it with jam.

11

Place on a serving plate, seam-side down. Swiss roll is best eaten on the day it is made.

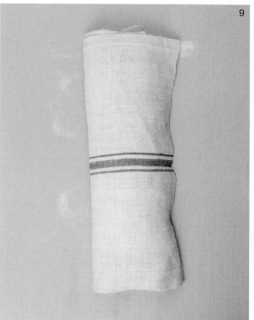

Iced Gingerbread Cookies

Preparation time: 20 minutes,
plus firming
Baking time: 9–11 minutes per batch
Makes about 14 gingerbread men,
or 24 smaller shapes

These happy little cookies are perfect
for an afternoon of baking with
children, as the dough can handle
plenty of squishing and rolling without
becoming tough. The level of spice
should please adult tastebuds too.
For a darker colour and bittersweet
flavour, replace the golden syrup
with black treacle.

_____

For the cookies

110 g butter, plus extra for greasing

200 g dark brown soft sugar

110 g golden syrup

1 egg

350 g plain flour, plus extra for rolling

1 tsp bicarbonate of soda

1 tbsp ground ginger

2 tsp ground cinnamon

¼ tsp salt

To decorate

1 egg or 2–3 tbsp lemon juice
   (see Tip)

200 g icing sugar

dragees or sparkles (optional)

1
Put the butter, sugar and syrup in a large pan, then gently heat until the butter has melted. Beat the egg.

2
Leave to cool for 5 minutes, then beat the egg into the pan. Mix the flour, bicarbonate of soda, spices and salt, then sift into the saucepan. Stir together to make a shiny dough.

3
Turn out the dough onto the work surface, split it in half, then knead briefly to make 2 smooth balls. Squash into flat discs, wrap well in clingfilm, then chill in the fridge until firm (this will take about 2 hours, or you can leave it overnight).

4
When ready to bake, grease 2 baking trays with a little butter, then line with baking parchment. Preheat the oven to 180°C (160°C fan/gas 4). Lightly flour the work surface and use a rolling pin to roll the dough out to 3 mm thick, or the thickness of a £1 coin. Cut out shapes and carefully lift them onto the lined trays, giving each one plenty of space. Squash together, re-roll and cut out the trimmings. You'll find the cookies come out of the cutter cleanly if you dip the cutter in a little flour first.

5

For softer cookies, bake for 9 minutes, or until golden all over (they will rise a little in the oven, then flatten out), or for cookies with snap, bake for 11 minutes, or until a little darker. Leave to cool for 5 minutes on the baking tray, then transfer to a wire rack to cool completely. Re-use the trays for the rest of the dough.

TREE DECORATIONS
To make your cookies into Christmas tree decorations, punch a hole in the cooked dough (while still hot) using a plastic drinking straw or small piping bag nozzle, or something like a pointy chopstick. Take care when handling the hot dough. Cool, then thread with ribbon to hang from the tree.

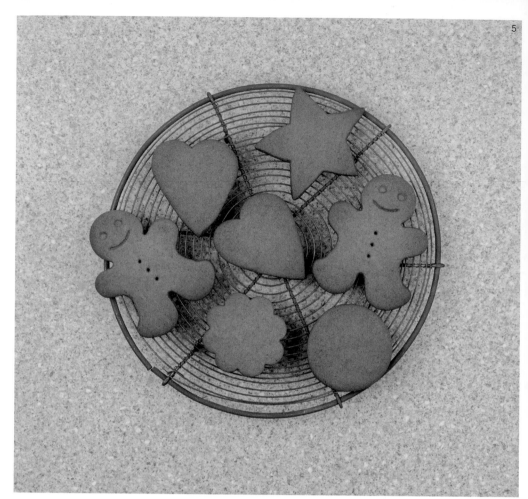

6

To make the icing, separate the egg (see page 127) and put the white in a clean bowl. Sift the icing sugar on top, stir it in slowly at first to incorporate, then beat well until smooth. Either drizzle teaspoons of the icing over your cookies to decorate, or spoon into a disposable piping bag or a food storage bag, snip off the very end and use it to pipe patterns. Decorate with dragees or sparkles, if you like.

ROYAL ICING
Icing made with egg white is known as royal icing. It has a bright whiteness to it, and sets very firmly. You can use shop-bought pasteurized egg whites if you are concerned about using raw eggs, or replace the egg white with lemon juice instead. Start with 2 tablespoons, then add more if needed.

7

Leave the icing to set for about 1 hour, or until firm and dry, before eating, hanging on the tree or packing into an airtight container.

Victoria Sandwich

Preparation time: 30 minutes
Baking time: 25 minutes
Makes 12 slices

This simple yet special family bake
is fit for the queen it's named after.
This recipe is a slight American slant
on the British classic, resulting
in layers that are tall and delicate,
but keep very well for three days,
and freeze well too.

For the cake

225 g soft butter, plus extra
    for greasing
300 g caster sugar
5 eggs, room temperature
285 g plain flour
2 tbsp cornflour
1 tbsp baking powder
¼ tsp salt
120 ml milk, at room temperature
1 tsp vanilla paste or extract
2 tbsp vegetable oil

For the buttercream filling

100 g soft butter
150 g icing sugar, plus extra
    for dusting
1 tsp vanilla extract or paste
1 tsp milk (if needed)
150 g strawberry jam

1

Preheat the oven to 180°C (160°C fan/gas 4). Use a little butter to grease two 20-cm round sandwich tins with removable bases, then line the bases with circles of baking parchment. Put the butter and sugar in a large bowl, then beat with an electric mixer until creamy and very pale.

2

Crack the eggs into a measuring jug. Pour 1 egg into the bowl with the creamed butter and sugar, then beat until it looks fluffy and light. Add the next egg and repeat. If the batter starts to look a little slimy at any point, beat in 1 tablespoon of the flour.

3

Stir the flour, cornflour, baking powder and salt together in a bowl. Put the milk, vanilla and oil in the eggy jug (to save washing another dish). Sift half of the flour on top of the batter, then fold in the milk mixture using a spatula or large metal spoon. Finish with the rest of the flour mixture and keep folding until you have a thick, smooth batter. A big blob of batter should drop (but not slide) away from the spatula if you give it a little shake. If it seems to cling on, then the batter may be a little dry; add 1 tablespoon more milk.

SHORTCUT?

If you want to make this cake more quickly, cream the butter and sugar together as in step 1, then add the rest of the ingredients, plus an extra 1 teaspoon baking powder, and beat them in with the electric mixer, taking care not to overwork the batter once it looks smooth and creamy. Cakes made this way can have a slightly less delicate texture and a lower rise, but if you're in a hurry, then go for it.

4

Scrape the batter into the prepared tins and smooth the tops. For a nice, even cake, try to ensure each one has more or less the same amount in it.

5

Bake for 25 minutes, or until the cakes are golden, have risen, spring back to the touch and a skewer inserted into the centre comes away clean. If the cakes are browning unevenly, they can be safely turned around after about 15 minutes, or once they have risen evenly and the surface looks dry. Be quick while you do this, to preserve heat in the oven. Leave to cool in the tins for 10 minutes, then turn out. I like to peel the paper from the bottom, put this on the cooling rack crumb-side down, then put the cakes on top.

6

Make the buttercream filling. Beat the butter until very soft. Sift in the icing sugar, add the vanilla, then gradually work the sugar in before increasing the beater speed and beating until smooth, pale and creamy. If it seems stiff, add 1 teaspoon milk.

7

Put one of the sponges on a serving plate, then spread with the buttercream. Top with the jam.

8

Sandwich with the second sponge, then sift a little more icing sugar over the top.

TRY IT WITH WHIPPED CREAM
Whip 250 ml double cream with 1 teaspoon vanilla and 1–2 tablespoons icing sugar (to your taste), until thickened but not stiff. Spread the jam first, then top with the cream.

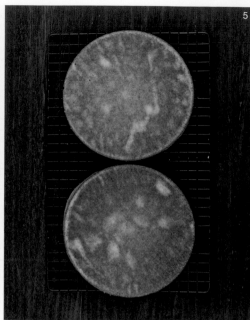

Chocolate & Nut
Banana Bread

Preparation time: 10 minutes
Baking time: about 1 hour 10 minutes
Makes 10 slices

There's no excuse not to use up
those spotty brown bananas hanging
around in the kitchen when the
method for making banana bread
is as straightforward as this. Mash,
fold and bake, and you're well on
your way to breakfast or teatime
happiness.

110 g butter

3 medium over-ripe bananas
    (to yield 250–300 g mashed fruit)

2 eggs

110 g maple syrup

85 g caster sugar

250 g plain flour

¼ tsp salt

2 tsp baking powder

85 g walnut pieces

60 g dark chocolate chips
    (or chopped dark chocolate)

1
Preheat the oven to 160°C (140°C fan/gas 3). Grease 23 x 12-cm loaf tin with a little of the butter, then line the base and two narrow ends of the tin with one long strip of baking parchment. Melt the butter in a saucepan. Using a fork, mash the bananas in a large bowl, until they're as smooth as possible.

2
Pour the melted butter into the bananas, then add the eggs and maple syrup. Beat everything together with the fork until the eggs are really well broken up. Mix the sugar, flour, salt and baking powder in a bowl, then sift onto the banana mixture. Using a spatula, fold in the flour mixture to make a smooth cake batter. Fold in most of the nuts and chocolate chips, saving a few to sprinkle on the top. Pour the batter into the tin, then sprinkle the reserved nuts and chocolate over the top.

3
Bake for 1 hour 10 minutes, or until the cake is golden, has risen well and a skewer inserted into the middle comes out clean, or with a few damp crumbs attached. The time can vary depending on how ripe your bananas are, as riper bananas will make a looser batter. Leave to cool in the tin for 15 minutes or so, then lift it out onto a cooling rack. Serve warm or cold, thickly sliced, and spread with butter, if you like.

IT'S A KEEPER
The cake will keep in an airtight container for up to 5 days, and can be frozen. To revive less-than-perfect banana bread, toast it lightly, or warm gently in the oven or microwave.

Lemon & Raisin Pancakes

Preparation time: 5 minutes
Cooking time: 15 minutes
Makes about 16 with the raisins,
12 without

Griddle cakes, drop scones, Scotch
pancakes – whatever you call them,
these fluffy treats are great for any
time of day: breakfast, brunch or
when the kids are home from school
and hungry. I like mine with lemon
and raisins, but the plain batter is
great cooked up with blueberries
too, or stacked high with crisp
bacon and maple syrup.

175 g plain flour

1½ tsp baking powder

½ tsp bicarbonate of soda

2 tbsp sugar

¼ tsp salt

1 lemon

250 g buttermilk (or see Tip)

2 tbsp milk

1 tsp vanilla extract

1 egg

85 g raisins or sultanas (optional)

about 2 tbsp vegetable oil

butter and maple syrup, to serve
    (optional)

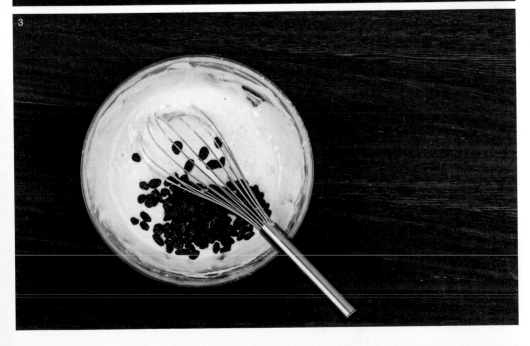

1

If you're planning to serve the pancakes all at once, rather than in batches straight from the pan, preheat the oven to 140°C (120°C fan/gas 1), and put a plate in to warm. Put the flour, baking powder and bicarbonate of soda in a large bowl. Add the sugar and salt, then whisk together to combine. Finely grate in the zest of the lemon.

WHY WHISK?
I often use a whisk instead of a sieve when all the dry ingredients are a similar texture (it wouldn't work with lumpier soft brown sugar in the bowl, for example). The whisk mixes and aerates, and there's a bit less to clean at the end of cooking.

2

Make a well in the centre of the flour, then add the buttermilk, milk and vanilla, and crack in the egg.

CAN'T FIND BUTTERMILK?
Mix 240 ml milk with 2 tablespoons lemon juice and leave to stand for 5 minutes. Use it in place of the buttermilk. You won't need the extra 2 tablespoons milk.

3

Using the whisk, start to mix the flour into the egg and buttermilk; keep going until everything is incorporated, then beat well to make a thick, smooth batter. Stir in the raisins, if using.

4

Put a large non-stick frying pan or flat griddle over a medium heat and add 1 teaspoon of the vegetable oil. Let it heat for a few seconds, swirl it to coat the pan, then add tablespoons of the batter to the pan, spaced well apart. The mixture should sizzle as soon as it hits the pan, and spread out a little. Nudge it around with the spoon to make neatish circles. Cook for 1 minute on the first side, or until bubbles start to appear and a few of them pop on the surface of the pancakes. Keep the heat steady.

5

Using a spatula, flip the pancakes over to reveal golden bottoms (starting with the one you first poured, so that they all have the same cooking time), and cook for another 30 seconds–1 minute, or until they have puffed in the middle and feel springy when pressed. Eat them while they're hot or remove from the pan, transfer to a plate and keep warm in the oven while you cook the rest.

GETTING AHEAD
Buttermilk pancakes are easy to reheat. Give them a few seconds in the microwave, toast under the grill or in a toaster, or wrap in foil and reheat in the oven at 180°C (160°C fan/gas 4) for 10 minutes. I like them cold, too.

6

Serve the warm pancakes with a little softened butter, a drizzle of maple syrup, and a squeeze from the lemon, if you like.

Rocky Road

Preparation time: 10 minutes,
plus setting time
Makes 16 squares

OK, this isn't strictly speaking
baking, but I couldn't leave out
such an all-round people-pleaser
of a recipe. I like to use gingernuts
in my rocky road, which give it a
spicy edge, but really any crunchy
biscuit will do, such as digestives,
Rich Tea or even Oreos for a double
chocolate hit.

55 g butter, plus extra for greasing
400 g dark chocolate, around
   60% cocoa solids
2 tbsp golden syrup
a pinch of salt
125 g mixed nuts
175 g crunchy biscuits
100 g marshmallows
85 g plump raisins, or other
   dried fruit
1 tbsp icing sugar

1
Use a little butter to grease a 23-cm shallow square tin or brownie pan, then line it with baking parchment. To melt the chocolate, first half-fill a medium pan with water and bring it to a simmer. Break the chocolate into squares and cut the butter into pieces, then put them in a large heatproof bowl. Sit the bowl over the pan of water, making sure that the bowl doesn't touch the water. (This is sometimes called a bain marie or double boiler.)

CHOOSING CHOCOLATE
If you can't find 60% cocoa content chocolate, use 200 g 50% cocoa chocolate (most supermarket 'Belgian' dark chocolate is around this percentage), plus 200 g 70% cocoa chocolate, and melt them together.

2
With the pan over a very low heat, let the chocolate and butter melt together, stirring now and again, until smooth and silky. Now stir in the syrup and salt and take the bowl off the heat.

3
While you wait for the chocolate to melt, roughly chop any larger nuts (such as brazils, if there are some in your mix). Crush or break the biscuits into smaller chunks. Snip the marshmallows in half.

4

Scoop about 8 tablespoons of the chocolate from the bowl and set aside. Toss all of the biscuit chunks, nuts, marshmallows and raisins, or whatever you are using, into the rest of the chocolate and stir well with a spatula until everything is well coated.

5

Spread the rocky road mixture into the tin, then add the 'tarmac': that is, spoon the reserved chocolate over the mixture to cover. It won't be perfectly smooth, but that's all part of the charm.

6

Let the rocky road chill in the fridge for about 3 hours, or longer if you like, until very firm. Remove from the tin, peel off the paper from the edges, cut into squares and dust with the icing sugar.

7

Store in the fridge or a cool place for up to 3 days.

TURKISH ROAD
Swap half the marshmallows for pieces of Turkish delight.

ROMAN ROAD
For an Italian panforte-inspired twist, replace half the raisins with finely chopped crystallized orange peel. Use amaretti biscuits and add 1 teaspoon ground cinnamon and ½ teaspoon ground nutmeg, plus a pinch of ground cloves, if you like.

Vanilla Fruit Scones

Preparation time: 15 minutes
Baking time: 12 minutes
Makes 10

A perfectly fluffy scone is a simple pleasure: quick and thrifty to make, but so delicious, especially when served just warm with cream or butter and a good dollop of jam or lemon curd. The most important thing to remember is not to knead the dough, which will quickly make your scones heavy.

400 g plain flour, plus extra
   for dusting
2 tsp baking powder
¼ tsp bicarbonate of soda
¼ tsp salt
100 g cold butter
60 g caster sugar
85 g sultanas or your choice
   of dried fruit (optional)
225 ml milk
2 tsp lemon juice
1 tsp vanilla extract
1 egg

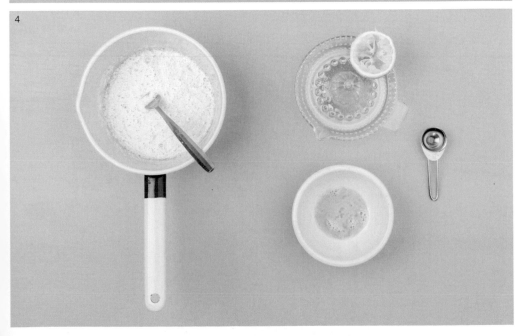

1

Preheat the oven to 220°C (200°C fan/gas 7). Put a large baking tray in the oven to heat up. Mix the flour, baking powder, bicarbonate of soda and salt, then sift into a large bowl. Cut the butter into cubes and add it to the bowl.

2

Rub the cold butter into the flour until it looks like fine breadcrumbs. If you have a food processor, simply process the butter into the dry ingredients instead, then tip into a large bowl.

COLD BUTTER

Fluffy, light scones need to be made with really cold butter. If it's a hot day and the butter begins to feel greasy as you rub it in, pop the bowl in the fridge for 10 minutes before continuing.

3

Stir in the sugar, and the dried fruit if you're using it. I've made this a separate step because I've forgotten to add the sugar so many times when making scones, and I'm determined that you won't do the same!

4

Heat the milk in a small pan (or in the microwave for a few seconds) until warm, then add the lemon juice and vanilla. Leave to sit for a few minutes until it turns a little bit lumpy. Beat the egg, then add 2 tablespoons of it to the lumpy milk mixture. Set the rest of the egg aside.

MILK OR BUTTERMILK?

Souring the milk lightens the dough by activating the bicarbonate of soda and boosting the rise. You can add 185 g buttermilk or yoghurt instead, and loosen with 4 tablespoons milk. Omit the lemon juice, but still use the egg.

5

Pour the soured milk evenly over the dry ingredients, working it into the flour with a table knife. Keep mixing until all the liquid is incorporated and you have a soft, rough dough. Don't worry if you miss a few crumbs at the bottom of the bowl; it's best not to overmix it.

6

Flour your hands and the work surface thoroughly. Turn the dough out onto it and sprinkle a little flour on top. Fold the dough over itself a couple of times just to smooth it a little (it's essential not to overwork it at this point), then pat it into a 3-cm thick round. Try to make sure the smoothest part of the dough ends up being the top.

7

Using a 6-cm round cookie cutter, cut out 6 scones. Dip the cutter into some flour between each cut to stop it sticking. Don't twist the cutter in the dough – the aim is to have a good, clean cut. Carefully press the remaining dough together and cut out the rest; remember not to overwork it.

8

Brush the tops of the scones with some of the remaining egg.

9

Remove the hot baking tray from the oven and sprinkle it with flour. Carefully place the scones on it, spacing them out evenly. The heat will give the scones a head start.

10

Bake for 12 minutes, or until the scones are golden and well risen, and sound hollow when tapped on the bottom. You may need to turn the tray around after 8 minutes to ensure an even colour. Cool on a wire rack. For a softer crust, wrap in a clean, dry tea towel before cooling.

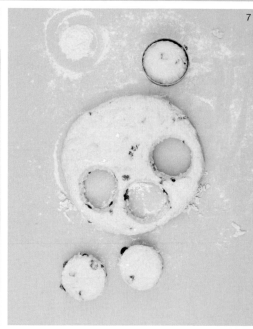

Malted Milk Chocolate Birthday Cake

Preparation time: 30 minutes
Baking time: 30 minutes
Makes 16 generous or 32
small pieces

There can be a lot of pressure to provide a homemade birthday cake that everyone will enjoy. This no-stress traybake keeps well if you want to get ahead, and is deliciously chocolatey but not too rich. It's easily cut into squares once the candles have been blown out.

For the cake

140 g soft butter

350 g plain flour

25 g good-quality cocoa powder

2 tbsp malted milk powder,
    such as Horlicks

1 tsp bicarbonate of soda

2 tsp baking powder

¼ tsp salt

300 g light brown soft sugar

300 ml milk

150 ml vegetable oil

1 tsp vanilla extract

For the frosting

200 g dark chocolate,
    about 50% cocoa solids

120 ml milk

25 g cocoa powder

2 tbsp malted milk powder

140 g soft butter

250 g icing sugar

a handful of chocolate sweets,
    and candles

1
Preheat the oven to 180°C (160°C fan/gas 4). Make the cake batter first. Put the butter in a saucepan and melt it gently. Using a pastry brush, use a little of the butter to grease a 23 x 33-cm traybake tin. Line the tin with baking parchment.

2
Mix the flour, cocoa, malted milk powder, bicarbonate of soda, baking powder and salt, then sift into a large bowl. Add the sugar and break up any lumps with your fingers. Make a well in the centre of the dry ingredients, pushing most of it to the sides of the bowl. Whisk the milk, oil and vanilla into the melted butter and pour them into the well.

3
Using the whisk, mix the flour mixture into the well, slowly at first. Once mixed, give it a good beat until smooth and evenly blended. Pour into the prepared tin.

4
Bake for 30 minutes, until the cake has risen, is firm and slightly shrunken from the sides. A skewer inserted into the centre should come out clean. Leave in the tin for 10 minutes, then turn out onto a cooling rack and cool completely.

5
For the frosting, break the chocolate into a heatproof bowl and place it over a pan of barely simmering water, making sure the bowl doesn't touch the water. Let the chocolate melt for about 5 minutes, stirring once or twice until smooth. Alternatively, microwave in 20-second bursts, stirring each time. Leave to cool a little.

NO EGGS?
This cake is egg-free, in case you wondered.

6

Heat the milk in a small saucepan or the microwave until steaming hot. Sift the cocoa and malted milk powder into a large bowl, then slowly stir in the hot milk to make a smooth paste. Leave to cool for a few minutes.

7

Now add the butter to the paste, sift in the icing sugar, and beat together with an electric mixer until very creamy. Follow with the melted, cooled chocolate, to make a silky, soft frosting.

8

Transfer the cooled cake to a board or large, flat plate, then spread the frosting all over it. It will firm a little as it cools, so try to create your swoops and swirls fairly quickly.

9

Sprinkle the cake with the sweets and top with coloured candles. Let the frosting set for a little while if you can, although it's delicious – if a little more messy – eaten straightaway too. The cake can be made up to 2 days ahead and kept in a cool place, well wrapped, or, if frosted, loosely covered on its board.

PATRIOTIC CAKE
For all the patriotic types out there, how about arranging the decorations in the colours of your national flag?

HALLOWEEN CAKE
Choose insect sweets and other gruesome things to top the cake, or stand long, thin biscuits up in the frosting, to look like gravestones.

EASTER CAKE
Scatter the frosting with pastel-coloured chocolate eggs.

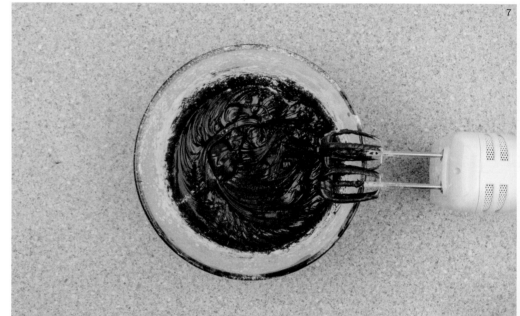

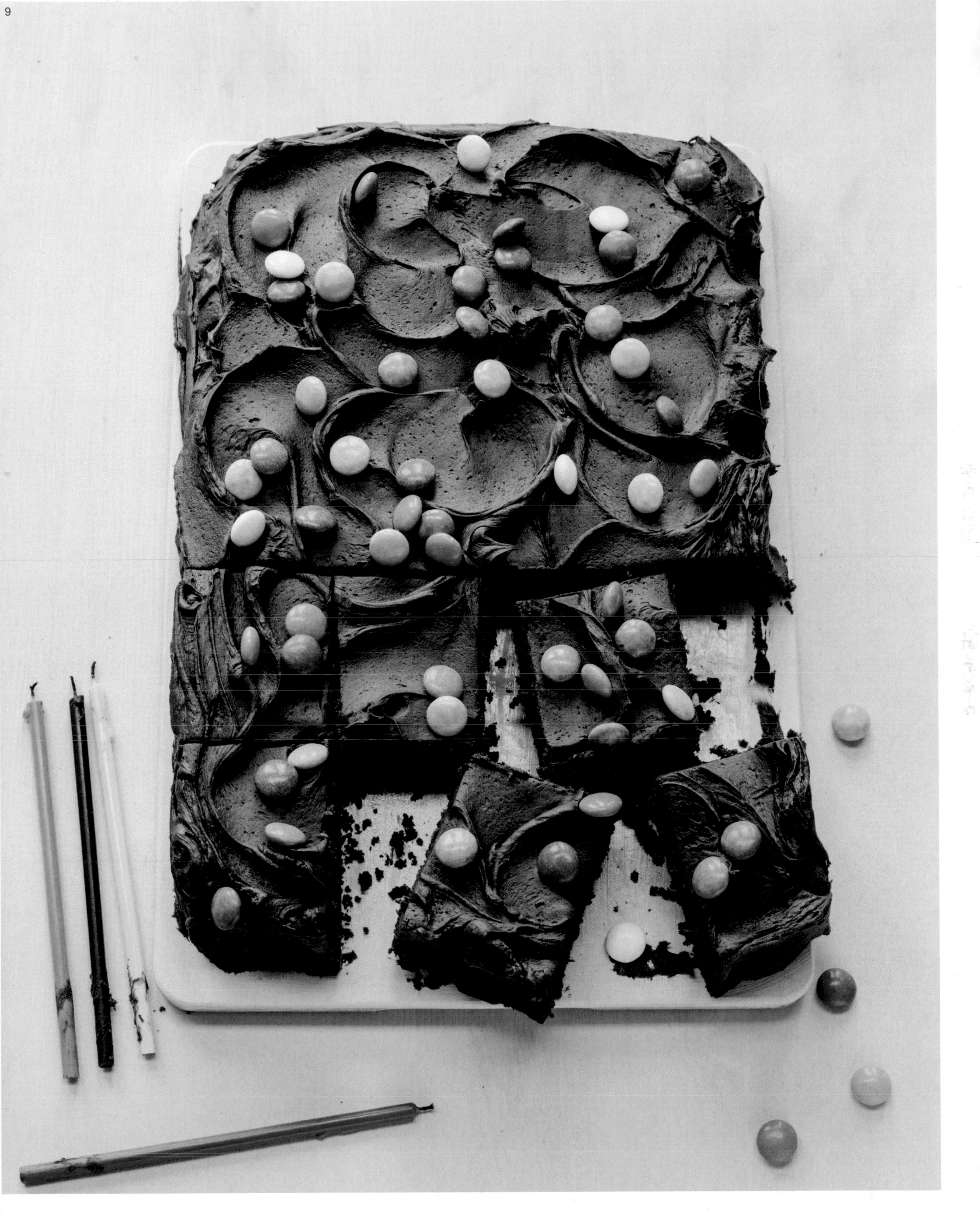

Classic Crusty Bread

Preparation time: 20 minutes,
plus rising and proving time
Baking time: 25–30 minutes
Makes 1 large loaf

Baking a loaf of bread from scratch
has to be one of the most satisfying
tasks ever. There's little to prevent
novice or rusty bakers from turning
out a loaf to be proud of, no matter
how much time you have to spare.
Most people are hooked after one
loaf, which is why I've included
a few easy variations to turn your
hand to next (see page 72).

500 g strong white bread flour,
   plus extra for dusting
2 tsp fast-action yeast
1 tsp sugar
2 tsp salt
about 300 ml warm water
2 tbsp olive oil, plus extra
   for greasing

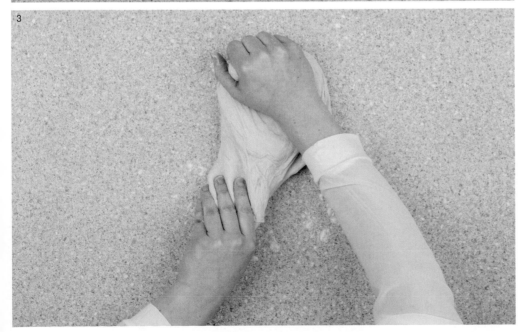

1
Put all the dry ingredients in a large bowl. Mix the water with the oil. The water should be pleasantly warm, but nowhere near hot; excess heat can kill the yeast.

2
Mix the dry ingredients together and, while stirring, pour in the water and oil. Keep working everything together until most of the dry flour has disappeared. The dough will be rough and a little sticky.

GETTING THE RIGHT TEXTURE
If a dough doesn't form, add a splash more water. A wetter dough will produce a tastier loaf in the end, and flours can differ a lot in moisture content, depending on their age, the weather and where the wheat was grown.

3
Dust the work surface with flour, then turn the dough out onto it. Flour the top of the dough and your hands, then begin to knead. Avoid adding too much flour as you knead. If the dough really sticks to the surface a lot, scrape away any bits with a knife, wash and dry your hands and start again, dusting the surface, the dough and your hands with a little more flour.

HOW TO KNEAD
As long as the dough is stretched and folded enough to make it springy and smooth, it doesn't really matter what your kneading technique is. I push the dough down with my left hand, grip it with my right and push it away. Then fold the dough back over itself, rotate it a quarter turn and repeat. If you have a stand mixer with a dough hook (or some food processors have dough 'blades'), that's a good – but less therapeutic – time saver.

4

Keep going until the dough feels very springy or elastic and silky smooth. To test if it's ready, gather it into a ball, tucking all the edges into the middle. Turn the ball over to reveal the smooth side. Keeping the dough pinched into a ball shape with one hand, press into it with the other hand. If the indent made by your finger stays there, it's not ready. If it springs out again, you're ready to move on.

5

Now leave the dough to rise. Grease a large bowl with 1 tablespoon oil, add the dough, then turn it around in the oil a few times to coat. Cover with clingfilm. You can also use a tea towel to cover the bowl, or grease a large food storage bag, pop the dough into it and seal it, leaving plenty of room for rising.

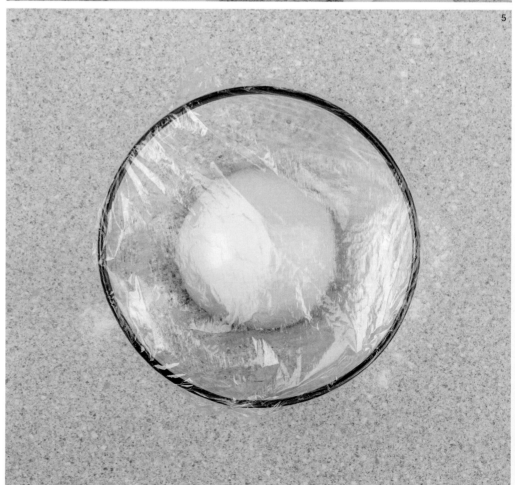

6
Leave the dough in a warm (but not hot) place for about an hour, or until doubled in size.

OVERNIGHT RISING
I often make the bread dough the night before, then leave it in the fridge overnight instead of in a warm place. Letting it rise more slowly means that the bread has a more complex flavour; let it come up to room temperature the next day, then continue.

7
Turn out the pillowy dough onto a floured surface, then press it out into a rectangle that's about the size of a piece of A4 paper. Do not knead it, or it will become stretchy again, and difficult to shape. Fold the bottom of the rectangle up, and the bottom half down, to make a sort of sausage. Pinch the edges together firmly.

8

Dust a baking tray with flour, then lift the dough onto it, smooth side up. Pat it back into shape if needed. Loosely cover with oiled clingfilm or the tea towel, then leave to rise again (it's known as proving at this stage) for 30 minutes, or until almost doubled in size. Poke the side of the dough; it doesn't spring back, it's ready to bake. Preheat the oven to 220°C (200°C fan/gas 7).

9

Sprinkle the top of the bread with more flour, then slash the top with a sharp knife. This is important, as it gives the bread somewhere to 'grow' in the oven.

10

Bake for 25–30 minutes, or until well risen, golden and crisp. When you think it's ready, double check by carefully turning the bread over. Tap the base; it should sound hollow. If not, bake for 10 more minutes. Leave to cool, open to the air for a crusty crust, or wrapped in a clean tea towel for a soft crust.

WHOLEMEAL SEEDED BREAD
Swap half the flour for wholemeal bread flour plus 3 tablespoons mixed seeds. You may need to add a little more liquid; try milk instead of water. Sprinkle with more seeds before slashing and baking.

ROSEMARY FOCACCIA
Press the risen dough into a 23 x 33-cm tin and prove. Just before baking, poke holes all over the dough, scatter with fresh rosemary sprigs and flaky sea salt, then drizzle with extra-virgin olive oil. Bake until risen and golden.

PIZZA BASES
Cut the risen dough into 4 pieces, roll out thinly on large baking trays, add the toppings, then bake at 240°C (220°C fan/gas 9) until crisp.

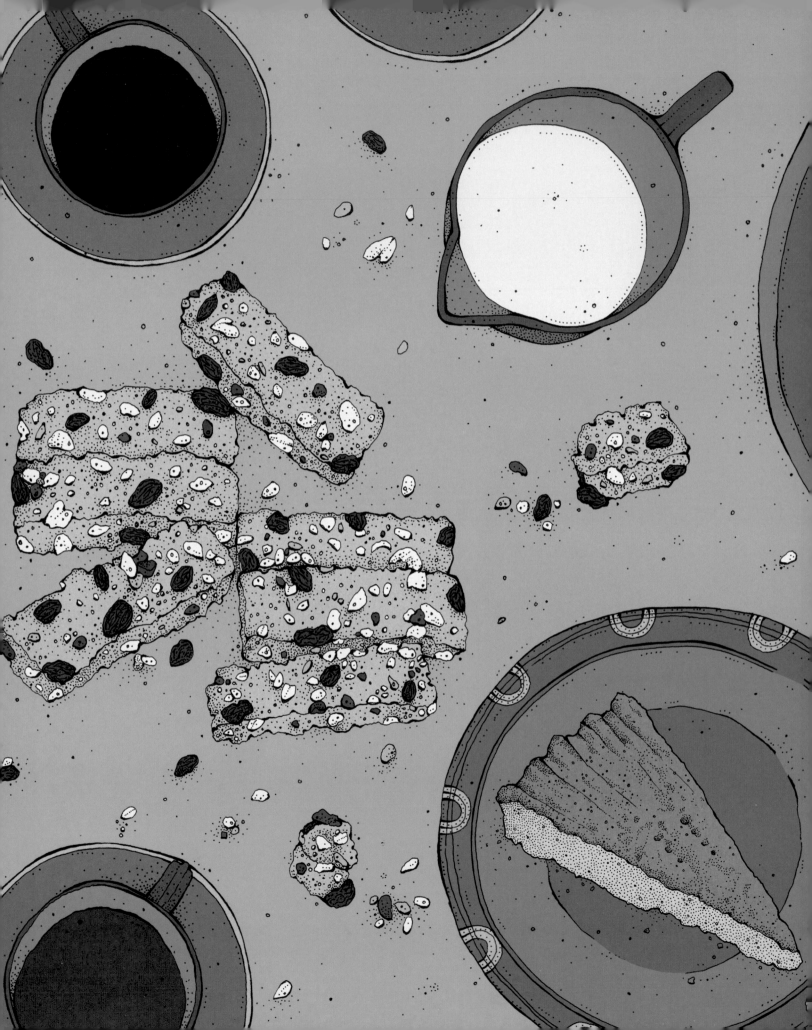

MORNING COFFEE
&
AFTERNOON TEA

Classic Shortbread

Preparation time: 15 minutes,
plus chilling
Baking time: 1 hour 10 minutes
Makes 12 pieces

Home-made shortbread takes
some beating. The quality of the
ingredients will make a difference in
the final flavour, so here's one recipe
for which I would invest in a slightly
more expensive brand of unsalted
butter. For shortbread with extra
crunch, substitute 80 g of the flour
with the same quantity of rice flour.

---

225 g soft butter
100 g caster sugar, plus extra
    for sprinkling
¼ tsp salt
1 tsp vanilla extract
280 g plain flour

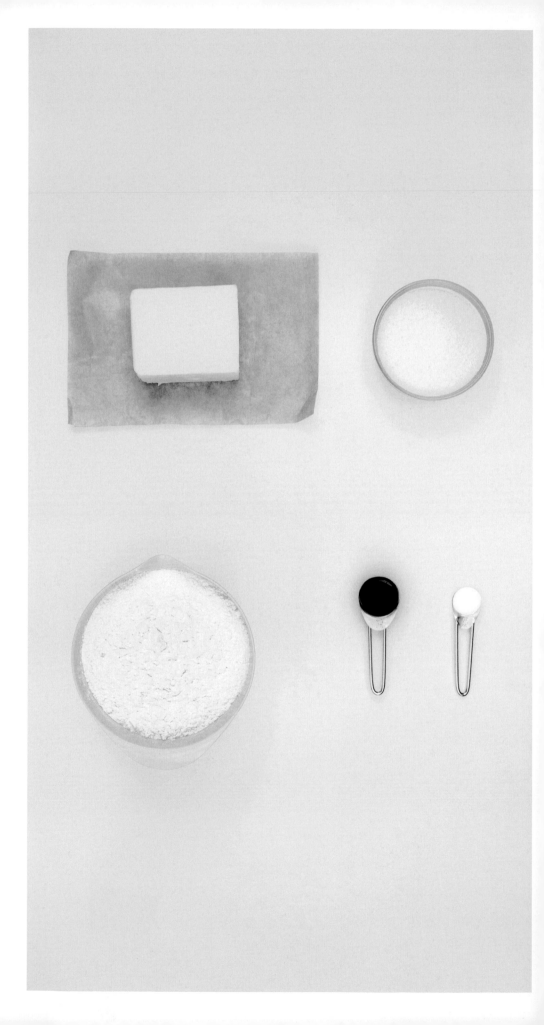

1

2

3

4

1
Prepare a 23-cm round fluted tart tin by greasing right into the ribs with a little of the butter. Put the rest of the butter in a large bowl and beat well with a wooden spoon or an electric mixer until creamy and very pale.

2
Add the sugar, salt and vanilla extract and beat again until even creamier and paler.

3
Sift the flour into the bowl. Using a spatula, gently fold and cut the flour in to the mixture to make an evenly blended dough. Don't overdo it: the less you mix, the more tender your shortbread will be.

4
Press the dough into the tin, then smooth it with the back of a spoon. If you find the spoon is dragging a little on the surface, sprinkle a little flour over the top and have another try. Any rough bits at the very edges of the tin can be pressed flat with your fingertips.

DIFFERENT TINS?
If you'd like to make this in an ordinary 23-cm round cake tin, that's fine, or you can press it into an 20-cm square tin instead, and cut the shortbread into rectangles. A tin with a removable bottom makes it easier to take the cooked shortbread out, but it isn't essential. The cooking time will be the same.

For a quicker version, roll the dough into a sausage about 6 cm across, wrap in clingfilm and chill in the freezer until firm. Slice into 1-cm rounds, then bake on a parchment-lined baking tray at 180°C (160°C fan/gas 4) for 20–25 minutes, or until golden.

5

Mark the edge of the shortbread with the tines of a fork, then cut the dough into 12 wedges. I do this in quarters first, then cut each quarter into three, to get nicely even pieces. Prick each piece of shortbread twice, going right to the base of the tin. Chill the shortbread for 20 minutes (or longer if you like), until very firm. Preheat the oven to 160°C (140°C fan/gas 3) while the shortbread chills.

6

Bake for 1 hour 10 minutes, or until golden and sandy all across the top. If you've used rice flour it might take a little less time, so check after 1 hour. Leave to cool in the tin for 5 minutes, then re-mark the wedges and fork holes. Sprinkle with 1–2 teaspoons sugar and leave to cool in the tin, on a rack.

7

Cut the shortbread into triangles to serve, then store in an airtight container for up to 1 week.

ORANGE SHORTBREAD
Add the finely grated zest of an orange to the mixture at step 2.

LAVENDER SHORTBREAD
Add 1 tablespoon chopped, unsprayed lavender flowers to the sugar and let it infuse for a few minutes before use. Rosemary works well too.

PECAN SHORTBREAD
Add 50 g chopped pecans to the dough. I like to add an extra pinch of salt to this one.

CHOCOLATE SHORTBREAD
Melt 50 g dark chocolate (70% cocoa solids). Separate the cooled biscuits on a rack, then drizzle with the chocolate instead of sprinkling with the extra sugar.

Courgette Cupcakes with Mascarpone Frosting

Preparation time: 20 minutes
Baking time: 20 minutes
Makes 12 cupcakes

Courgettes, like carrots in carrot cakes, add a soft freshness to these cupcakes rather than any particular flavour, and are well worth a try. A quick lemon drizzle ramps up the zesty flavour, and a luscious lemon curd mascarpone finishes them off beautifully.

For the cupcakes

200 g courgettes (about 1–2; smaller ones are better)
175 g soft butter, plus extra for greasing
1 lemon
150 g caster sugar, plus 1 tbsp extra
200 g plain flour (or see Tip)
2½ tsp baking powder
¼ tsp salt
3 eggs, room temperature
1 tbsp poppy seeds

For the frosting

150 g good-quality lemon curd
250 g mascarpone
2 tsp poppy seeds

1
Trim, then coarsely grate the courgettes, skins and all. You should have about 150 g. Spread them out between kitchen paper or on a clean tea towel and set aside for a few minutes while you get everything else ready.

2
Preheat the oven to 180°C (160°C fan/gas 4). Grease the holes of a 12-hole non-stick muffin tin, or use 12 deep paper cases in an ungreased tin if you prefer. Finely grate the zest from the lemon and squeeze the juice. Put the zest, 2 tablespoons juice and the butter and sugar in a large mixing bowl. Beat using an electric mixer or wooden spoon until creamy and pale.

3
Mix the flour, baking powder and salt together, then sift on top of the butter and sugar mixture. Crack in the eggs, then beat everything together until evenly blended. Try not to overwork the batter once the flour has gone in.

TRY A DIFFERENT FLOUR
These cupcakes are also delicious made with spelt flour, or a 50:50 mix of spelt and plain, or wholemeal and plain. Both give a slightly nuttier taste and texture to the end result. Wholemeal flour can absorb more liquid than ordinary flour, so add 1 tablespoon milk if the batter seems too thick.

4

Fold in the poppy seeds and grated courgettes, then spoon into the prepared tin. The holes will seem fairly full, which is fine.

5

Bake for 20 minutes, or until they have risen and are golden, and a skewer inserted into one of the middle cakes comes out clean. Mix the rest of the lemon juice with the extra sugar and let it melt together, stirring occasionally, while the cakes cook. Poke holes in the tops of the cakes with a cocktail stick and spoon the syrup over them. Leave to cool for 10 minutes, then remove to a cooling rack.

6

To make the frosting, put the lemon curd and mascarpone in a large bowl and beat with a wooden spoon or spatula until smooth and evenly blended. Dollop it onto the cooled cakes just before eating and swirl with a spoon or small palette knife.

7

Sprinkle with the poppy seeds to finish. The cupcakes are best enjoyed fresh, but keep any leftover cakes in a cool place or in the fridge once the frosting has been added.

Jaffa Marble Loaf

Preparation time: 30 minutes
Baking time: 55–60 minutes
Makes 8–10 slices

With its hidden swirls of chocolate and zesty orange, this is a fun cake to make, and to cut in front of a hungry audience. The dark chocolate topping keeps the balance in favour of bitter rather than sweet; for young children you may want to use milk chocolate instead of dark.

For the cake

175 g soft butter, plus extra
    for greasing
1 large orange
175 g caster sugar
175 g plain flour
¼ tsp salt
1 tsp baking powder
3 eggs, room temperature
3 tbsp vegetable oil
2 tbsp cocoa powder

For the topping

100 g dark chocolate,
    70% cocoa solids
2 tbsp golden syrup

1
Grease a 23 x 12-cm loaf tin with butter, then line it with 2 strips of baking parchment that hang over the sides. Preheat the oven to 160°C (140°C fan/gas 3). Finely grate the zest from the orange, then squeeze the juice.

2
Put the butter, sugar and most of the orange zest in a large bowl. Using an electric mixer, beat together until pale and creamy.

3
Mix the flour, salt and baking powder, then sift them on top of the creamed mixture. Add the eggs and oil.

4
Beat everything together until smooth, adding 3 tablespoons of the orange juice to bring the batter to soft dropping consistency.

SOFT DROPPING CONSISTENCY
A spoonful of cake batter should drop easily into the bowl when given a gentle shake. If it resists, it's a sign that the batter is too stiff and will make a dry cake. To get a moist, tender cake, recipes often call for a liquid, in this case the orange juice, to be added after the flour has gone in. The amount of liquid you need will depend on the recipe and the type and age of the flour you are using. The oil in this recipe also helps to keep it moist, so it's ideal for making ahead for a bake sale, or the kitchen cupboard.

5
Spoon half the cake batter into another bowl, then sift in the cocoa powder and mix until evenly blended. If it seems dry compared to the orange batter, add another tablespoon of orange juice.

6

Spoon the chocolate and orange cake batters into the tin in alternating spoonfuls until both bowls are empty. Stir a skewer or chopstick through the batter a couple of times to ripple the blobs together and encourage swirls in the middle of the cake.

7

Bake for 55–60 minutes, or until it is golden and has risen all the way to the middle. Insert a skewer into the centre of the cake; if it comes out clean, it is ready. Cool in the tin for 10 minutes, then lift out using the lining paper and cool on a wire rack. For the topping, melt the chocolate in a heatproof bowl over a pan of water, or in the microwave (see page 119). Stir in the syrup and reserved orange zest.

8

Spread the topping over the cooled cake, then let it set for an hour or so, until firm.

9

Slice the cake thickly and serve, or wrap and keep in an airtight container for up to 3 days.

MOCHA-CHOCOLATE
MARBLE LOAF
Dissolve 2 tablespoons instant coffee granules in 4 tablespoons hot water. Add 3 tablespoons to the base mixture instead of the orange, and 1 tablespoon in with the cocoa when you make the chocolate batter. Omit the orange zest from the topping. You could use coffee-flavoured chocolate, if you like.

Cherry-Almond Streusel Slice

Preparation time: 20 minutes, or
longer if you make your own pastry
Baking time: 40–45 minutes
Cuts into 15 or 18 bars

Cherries and almonds are a classic
pairing, but I've tried this with
raspberries, sliced apple and chunks
of stone fruit (such as apricots or
peach) too, each with great results.
The contrast between the rich
almond cake, pastry and fruit
is what makes this irresistible.

For the base and streusel topping

1 quantity sweet shortcrust pastry,
   made with all butter (see page
   210 and Tip), or use 350 g
   ready-made

For the cake layer

65 g plain flour, plus extra
   for dusting
200 g soft butter
200 g caster sugar
4 eggs
½–1 tsp almond extract (depending
   how almondy you like things)
100 g ground almonds
½ tsp baking powder
¼ tsp salt
150 g cherry or raspberry jam
200 g whole cherries, or 150 g
   stoned (fresh, canned or frozen
   and defrosted)
a handful of flaked almonds

For the icing (optional)
75 g icing sugar
2–3 tsp lemon juice

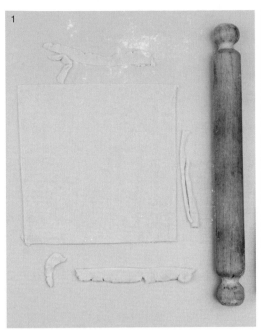

1

Preheat the oven to 180°C (160°C fan/gas 4) and put a flat baking tray in the oven to heat up. Cut one sixth of the dough from the block and set it aside in the fridge – this will be used for the topping later. Roll out the rest on a lightly floured surface until it is just bigger than the base of a 23-cm shallow square tin, then trim it to neaten the edges. Keep any trimmings to use later, and chill these too. Remove the stones from the cherries, if using fresh, and cut them in half.

ALL-BUTTER PASTRY
For a deliciously buttery crust you can use a total of 120 g butter to make the pastry on page 210, instead of the butter and vegetable shortening.

2

Push the pastry into the tin, letting it come a little way up the sides to make a rim of about 1 cm. If the pastry rips at all, just gently pinch it back together.

3

To make the cake layer, put the butter and sugar in a large bowl and beat together until creamy and paler. Don't worry about incorporating too much air – a wooden spoon is fine. Add the eggs, almond extract and ground almonds, then beat until everything is combined.

4

Mix the flour, baking powder and salt in a bowl, then sift it onto the batter. Stir it in until smooth.

5
Spread the jam over the pastry, then spread the cake batter on top. It doesn't matter if some of it spills over the top of the pastry and touches the side of the tin.

6
Sprinkle the prepared fruit over the cake batter, then tear the reserved pastry and trimmings over it to make a struesel top. Scatter with the flaked almonds.

7
Carefully slide the tin onto the baking tray in the oven. This will give a boost of heat to the bottom of the tin, helping the pastry base to cook thoroughly. Bake for 40–45 minutes, or until the cake has risen to the centre, is firm and a deep, glowing gold. Leave to cool in the tin. Once cooled, top with the icing. Sift the icing sugar and slowly stir in enough lemon juice to make a smooth, flowing icing, then drizzle it liberally over the cake, letting it run off the spoon.

8
Let the icing set, then cut into 15 or 18 bars. Keep in an airtight container in a cool place for up to 3 days.

BAKEWELL TART
For bakers with a taste for the classics, line a 23-cm fluted tart tin with the pastry, taking it right to the top of the tin (see page 194 for how to line a tin with pastry). Fill with the jam, batter and fruit, then scatter with the almonds. Bake as above, then drizzle with the icing and cut into wedges when cooled. Use halved glacé cherries instead of fresh fruit for the full effect.

Carrot Cake with Cream Cheese Frosting

Preparation time: 30 minutes
Baking time: 30–35 minutes
Makes 12 slices

Carrot cake is perfect as a first cake to make, since it's not only tasty, but also less likely to overcook and be dry, thanks to the water content in the carrots. If you'd like to make the cake in squares or cupcakes instead of layers, see the variations on page 94.

For the cake

100 g pecans
200 ml vegetable oil, plus extra
    for greasing
250 g plain flour
2 tsp baking powder
½ tsp bicarbonate of soda
2 tsp ground mixed spice
½ tsp salt
200 g light brown soft sugar
1 orange
3 eggs
300 g carrots
85 g raisins

For the frosting

110 g soft butter
300 g full-fat cream cheese, cold
½ tsp vanilla extract
100 g icing sugar

1

Preheat the oven to 180°C (160°C fan/gas 4). Spread the nuts over a baking tray and cook for 8–10 minutes, or until golden and toasty. Cool, then roughly chop. Toasting nuts will add an extra depth of flavour to the batter, but if you're in a hurry, just chop the nuts and use them as they are.

2

While you wait, get everything else ready. Grease two 20-cm round sandwich tins with removable bases with a little oil, then line the bases with baking parchment. Mix the flour, baking powder, bicarbonate of soda, spices and salt, then sift into a large bowl. Add the sugar and work it in with your fingers, breaking up any larger lumps, until evenly blended. Finely grate the zest of the orange into the bowl. Squeeze the juice for later.

HOW TO MIX YOUR SPICES
For a simple home-made ground mixed spice, combine 1 tablespoon ground cinnamon, 2 teaspoons ground ginger, ½ teaspoon each ground nutmeg and allspice and ¼ teaspoon ground cloves, if you have them. You'll have some left over for next time, too.

3

Crack the eggs into the measuring jug with the oil, add 2 tablespoons orange juice and beat together.

4

Trim, then coarsely grate the carrots and measure them to make sure you have 250 g. Pour the oil mixture into the dry ingredients and beat until smooth. Add most of the nuts, then the carrots and raisins, and stir until evenly blended. If the batter seems at all stiff, add 1 tablespoon more orange juice. Divide the batter between the prepared tins.

5

Bake for 30–35 minutes, or until the cakes are golden and have risen, and a skewer inserted into the centre comes out clean. Cool in the tins on a rack for 10 minutes, then turn out of the tins and cool completely.

6

To make the frosting, put the butter in a large bowl and beat well until creamy and totally smooth. Add the cream cheese and vanilla and beat until smooth and evenly blended. Now sift in the icing sugar and work it in gently with a spatula.

FOR PERFECT FROSTING
It's important that the butter and cream cheese are the correct temperatures, or the frosting can end up lumpy. If that happens, pass it through a sieve and no one will be any the wiser. Do not overwork it once the sugar has been added, as this can loosen the texture.

7

Put one of the cakes upside down on a serving plate, then use a palette knife to spread about a third of the frosting across it. Top with the other cake, then spread the remaining frosting over the top and the sides (see page 136 for guidance).

8

Sprinkle the reserved pecans over the top. The cake benefits from a little while in the fridge to settle. If it's a hot day, keep it there until you are ready to slice it.

CARROT TRAYBAKE
Use a 23 x 33-cm tin and bake for 40 minutes, or until a skewer comes out clean. Frost, then cut into squares.

CARROT CUPCAKES
Also makes 18 cupcakes. Bake for 20–25 minutes, then cool and frost.

Fudgy Cheesecake Brownies

Preparation time: 20 minutes
Baking time: 30–35 minutes
Makes 16

A swirl of cheesecake topping gives
these brownies a different look,
and a delicious, creamy contrast
to the dark fudginess beneath.
Prefer a simple brownie? Just leave
out the cheesecake topping and
jump to step 8. And yes, the batter
will give that shiny, papery crust
we all love. Turn the page for more
flavour options.

For the brownies

200 g butter, plus extra for greasing

200 g dark chocolate, about
    60% cocoa solids (see Tip)

4 eggs

300 g caster sugar

125 g plain flour

50 g cocoa powder

½ tsp salt

For the cheesecake topping

200 g full-fat cream cheese,
    room temperature

1 egg

2 tbsp caster sugar

1 tsp vanilla extract

1

Grease a 23-cm shallow square cake tin with a little butter, then line it with baking parchment. Preheat the oven to 180°C (160°C fan/gas 4). Make the brownie base first. Melt the butter in a medium saucepan. While you wait, break the chocolate into pieces, then add them to the melted butter, and take the pan off the heat.

CHOCOLATE IN COOKING
A good-quality 70% cocoa chocolate is often used for baking for its intense cocoa flavour. But it can sometimes seem a little sour and overwhelm a family-style treat like a brownie. My preference is to use a dark chocolate of around 60% cocoa, or a half-and-half mixture of 70% and 50%. This reduces the cost a little, too.

2

Let the chocolate melt until smooth, stirring now and again with a spatula.

3

Put the eggs and sugar in a large bowl. Using a whisk, beat together until frothy and a little thicker, just for 30 seconds or so.

4

Pour the melted butter and chocolate into the eggs and whisk to combine. Sift the flour, cocoa and salt into the bowl.

5

Beat together using your (already chocolatey) whisk, until smooth and thick. Scoop about 4 tablespoons of the batter from the bowl and set aside, then scrape the rest into the prepared tin and smooth the top.

6

Now make the topping. Put the cream cheese in a large bowl, add the egg, sugar and vanilla. Whisk until smooth and creamy.

7

Spoon the cheese over the brownie batter in the tin, then spread it into a thin layer using the back of the spoon or a spatula. Spoon the reserved brownie batter over the cheesecake topping. Drag a skewer or the tip of a knife through the cheesecake layer to create feathery swirls.

8

Bake for 30–35 minutes, or until the brownie has risen all over and jiggles just a little in the middle when you gently shake the tin. This is vital for a fudgy result. Leave to cool completely in the tin, then cut into squares. They'll keep in an airtight container for several days.

VARIATIONS
Add different flavours at step 5, and leave out the cheesecake topping.

Classic Walnut Brownies: Fold 100 g chopped walnuts into the batter.

Sour Cherry & White Chocolate Brownies: Fold in 50 g dried cherries and 50 g chopped white chocolate.

Peanut Butter Brownies: Warm 4 tablespoons peanut butter in a pan, then spoon it over the raw batter and swirl in with a knife.

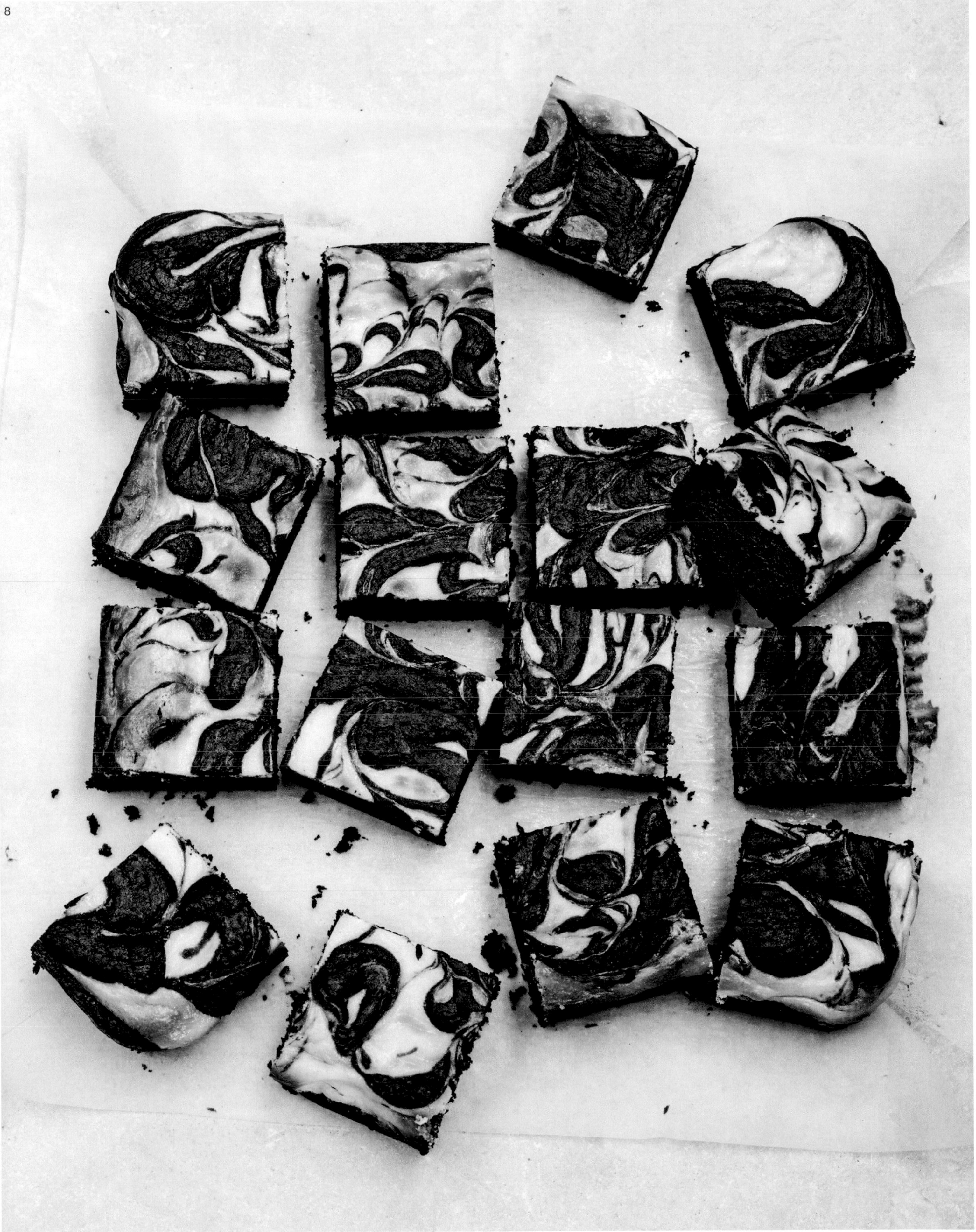

Lemon-Glazed Ginger Cake

Preparation time: 20 minutes
Baking time: 50 minutes
Makes 12 slices

Everyone who tried this cake fell in love with it, including me! Making cakes this way with black treacle guarantees a deliciously dense and sticky cake, which keeps very well in an airtight container for at least a week. Don't worry if you don't have a bundt tin – see the instructions for making it in an ordinary 23 x 33-cm tin over the page.

For the cake
180 ml vegetable oil, plus extra
    for greasing
100 g crystallized ginger
    (or use glacé ginger packed
    in syrup, drained)
300 g dark brown soft sugar
150 g black treacle
240 ml milk
3 eggs
1 lemon
300 g plain flour
1½ tsp bicarbonate of soda
1 tbsp ground ginger
1 tsp ground allspice
    (or use cinnamon)
¼ tsp salt

For the glaze
100 g icing sugar
about 2 tbsp lemon juice

1
Preheat the oven to 180°C (160°C fan/gas 4) and grease a 25-cm diameter bundt tin with a little oil, or use non-stick cooking spray. Chop the crystallized ginger into small pieces.

2
Put the dark brown sugar, treacle and milk in a large pan and let them melt gently together.

3
Take the pan off the heat, whisk in the oil to cool the mixture, then add the eggs and whisk until smooth. Finely grate in the zest of the lemon.

4
Mix the flour, bicarbonate of soda, spices and salt, then sift into a large bowl. Make a well in the centre by pushing the flour to the sides of the bowl, then pour in the wet ingredients. Add most of the chopped ginger, saving some for decoration later.

5

Mix the dry ingredients into the wet, going slowly at first. Once everything is mixed, give the batter a good beat with the whisk until smooth and evenly blended. Pour into the prepared bundt tin.

6

Bake for 35 minutes, by which point the cake should have risen all over and be dark golden; but don't open the oven door yet or it will sink. Turn the oven down to 160°C (140°C fan/gas 3) for a final 15 minutes of cooking. Test by inserting a skewer into the deepest part of the cake; it should come out clean. Put the tin on a wire rack and leave the cake to cool completely.

7

To decorate the cake, sift the icing sugar into a large bowl. Squeeze the lemon juice, then stir 4–5 teaspoons into the sugar until smooth. It needs to be thicker than you think, so see how it flows from the spoon before you add any more juice. Turn the cake out onto a serving plate, then drizzle with the icing.

8

Scatter the reserved chopped ginger over the cake, then let the icing set for at least 30 minutes.

NO BUNDT TIN?
No problem, simply make gingerbread fingers instead. Bake the cake in the same way, in a parchment-lined 23 x 33-cm baking tin, until a skewer inserted into the centre comes out clean. Drizzle with the glaze, or make a double batch with 200 g icing sugar and a few more teaspoons of lemon juice, then spread it thickly over the top of the cake. Leave to set, then cut into bars, wiping the knife clean before making each cut.

Skinny Blueberry Muffins

Preparation time: 15 minutes
Baking time: 25 minutes
Makes 12 muffins

Muffins are easy to grab and go,
but I always want something with at
least a nod to health in the morning.
This butter-less, fluffy muffin is
good enough to rival the one from
the coffee shop, without the guilt
trip. The sweetness from the apple
reduces the amount of sugar and
fat needed, and there's added fibre
from the fruit and flour, too.

For the muffins

1 lemon

240 ml milk

1 medium dessert apple

200 g plain flour

125 g wholemeal flour

1 tsp baking powder

1 tsp bicarbonate of soda

1 tsp ground mixed spice

½ tsp salt

125 g light brown soft sugar

80 ml vegetable oil

2 tsp vanilla extract

2 eggs

150 g blueberries (fresh are best
   but frozen are fine)

For the glaze (optional)

50 g icing sugar

2–3 tsp milk

1
Preheat the oven to 200°C (180°C fan/gas 6) and line a 12-hole muffin tin with deep paper cases. Grate the zest from the lemon (save this for later), then squeeze the juice from one half. Stir 1 tablespoon juice into the milk and leave to stand for a few minutes until it thickens and turns a bit lumpy.

2
Meanwhile, grate the apple with a coarse grater, skin and all.

3
Mix the flours, baking powder, bicarbonate of soda, spice and salt, then sift into a large bowl. This allows for the raising agents to be thoroughly mixed with the flour. Return the bran from the wholemeal flour, which will collect in the sieve, to the bowl. Stir in the sugar, then make a well in the middle. Beat the oil, vanilla and eggs into the now-lumpy milk.

4

Pour the liquid into the well.
Add the apple and berries too.

5

Stir the mixture together briefly to
make a rough batter. Don't worry if
there are still a few bits of dry flour
here and there.

6

Spoon generous heaped spoons
of batter into the lined tin, or use
an ice cream scoop, which helps
do the job very cleanly; about one
scoop per case. They will seem
quite full, but that's fine. Bake for
about 25 minutes, or until they have
risen well and are golden. Don't
open the oven until every muffin
has risen right to the centre.

7

Make the glaze, if you like. Sift the
icing sugar into a bowl, then slowly
beat in the milk, to make a smooth paste.
Stir in the reserved lemon zest.
Drizzle the glaze over the muffins.

8

Leave to cool, then eat the same day.

GET AHEAD
Muffins are always best baked fresh,
so why not bag the wet ingredients,
including the apple, and chill. Get
the dry ingredients ready in a bowl.
In the morning, combine the two
mixtures and get the muffins in the
oven in 2 minutes flat.

CHEESE & HAM CORNBREAD
MUFFINS
For a quick savoury option, switch
the wholemeal flour for fine cornmeal.
Use only 1 teaspoon sugar and omit
the vanilla, spice and fruit. Beat
2 teaspoons wholegrain mustard
into the soured milk, egg and 4
tablespoons oil. Stir in 50 g grated
mature Cheddar, 50 g chopped ham
and 100 g drained tinned sweetcorn.
Bake for 18 minutes.

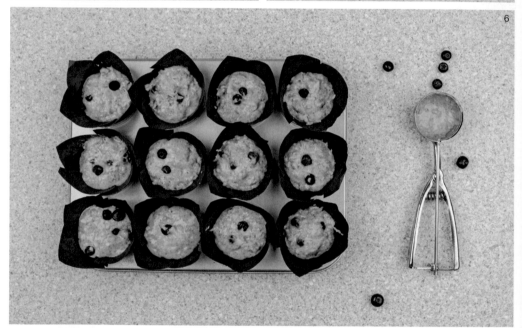

Fruity Granola Bars

Preparation time: 20 minutes
Baking time: 35 minutes
Makes 12 bars

These satisfying bars are packed
with good things to keep you going
until lunchtime, and the butter and
sugar have been kept to a minimum
with no loss of texture or flavour.
The recipe can be easily changed
to include your favourite dried fruit,
nuts and seeds. Quick-cooking
rolled oats are the best choice
for these bars because they stick
together nicely.

250 g porridge oats (not the
    jumbo ones)
50 g unsweetened desiccated
    coconut
75 g pumpkin or sunflower seeds
50 g flaked almonds
55 g butter, plus extra for greasing
100 g light brown soft sugar
a pinch of salt
160 g clear honey
85 g soft dried apricots
2 tbsp fruit juice (apple works well),
    or use water
140 g dried berries and cherries
    (or use raisins or other dried fruit)

1

Preheat the oven to 160°C (140°C fan/gas 3). Mix the oats, coconut, seeds and nuts on a large baking tray and bake for 15 minutes, stirring halfway through, until they smell toasty and are pale golden here and there. Meanwhile, grease a 23-cm shallow square baking tin, then line it with baking parchment. Put the butter, sugar, salt and honey in a large saucepan and melt them gently together to make a syrup. Chop the dried apricots, or snip them with scissors.

2

Pour the toasted oats, seeds and nuts into the pan, then add the fruit juice or water and the dried fruit. Stir well with a spatula until everything is evenly coated in the syrup. Press the granola into the baking tin and smooth it flat with the back of a spoon.

3

Bake for 35 minutes, or until golden all over, then leave to cool completely in the tin. Lift the baked slab of granola from the tin using the paper to help, then cut into bars using a large sharp knife. Re-wrap in clean baking parchment and keep in the tin or an airtight container for up to 1 week.

Caramel & Walnut Coffee Cake

Preparation time: 25 minutes
Baking time: 20–25 minutes
Makes 12 slices

A stalwart of British teashops and coffee mornings, this cake deserves a place in cake-lovers' hearts everywhere. I like to moisten the layers with strong coffee and finish with a crown of caramelized walnuts and frosting for a slightly flashier riff on the original.

For the cake

2 tbsp instant coffee granules,
     or 120 ml very strong coffee
250 g soft butter, plus extra
     for greasing
50 g walnut halves
250 g caster sugar, plus 2 tbsp extra
5 eggs, room temperature
2 tbsp milk
300 g plain flour
1 tbsp baking powder
¼ tsp salt

For the frosting and decoration
100 g caster sugar (optional)
50 g walnut halves
1 tbsp instant coffee granules
     (or 1 tbsp very strong coffee)
110 g soft butter
250 g icing sugar
1 tbsp maple syrup (optional)

1
Preheat the oven to 180°C (160°C fan/gas 4). If using instant coffee, dissolve it in 120 ml just-boiled water and set aside to cool. Use a little butter to grease two 20-cm round sandwich tins with removable bases, then line the bases with baking parchment. Finely chop the nuts.

2
Put the butter and sugar for the cake in a large bowl and beat with an electric mixer until creamy and pale. Crack in the eggs and add the milk. Mix the flour, baking powder and salt together, sift them over the eggs, then beat together until creamy.

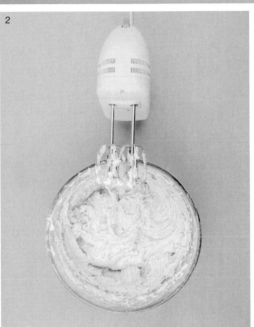

3
Using a spatula or large spoon, fold in the chopped walnuts and 5 tablespoons of the cooled coffee.

4
Spoon the batter into the prepared tins and level the tops. Bake for 20–25 minutes, or until it has risen, is golden, springs back to the touch, and a skewer inserted in the centre comes out clean.

5
Leave to cool in the tins for 10 minutes, then turn out and cool upside-down on a cooling rack. I like to peel the paper from underneath, put this on the cooling rack (cakey-side down), then put the cakes on top of it. This prevents them from sticking to the rack. Stir the extra sugar into the remaining coffee, let it dissolve, then drizzle this all over the cakes. Leave to cool completely.

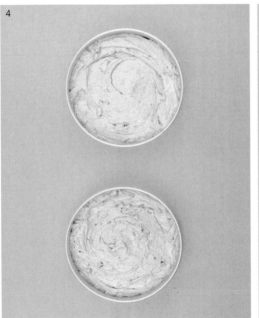

6

The frosting and topping can be simple, or less so, it's up to you. If you want the simple option, jump straight to step 8, use plain walnuts and add 1 tablespoon maple syrup to the recipe instead of using the caramel. Or, if you're with me on the caramel, read on: line a baking tray with baking parchment. Put the sugar in a small saucepan or small deep frying pan, and heat gently. It will start to look patchy here and there. Don't be tempted to stir it at this point or it could seize, becoming hard and opaque.

7

Carefully swirl the melted patches of sugar over the dry bits, returning to the heat occasionally, to make an even-coloured dark coppery caramel. If there are few bits of sugar left, now you can give it a quick stir. Stir the walnuts into the caramel, then use a fork to transfer them one by one to the lined tray to harden. When you've finished, add 1 tablespoon water to the pan and let it bubble to a runny, dark caramel.

8

If using instant coffee for the frosting, dissolve it in 1 tablespoon just-boiled water. Beat the butter until creamy, then gradually work in the icing sugar. Once all the dry sugar has disappeared, give it a good whizz until pale and fluffy. Add the coffee and 1 tablespoon of the caramel (or maple syrup), then beat again.

9

Spread the frosting on the top of each cake, stack them on a serving plate and top with the walnuts. The cake will keep well in an airtight container for 3 days or so. The layers can be frozen for up to a month, and the frosting and nuts can be made a few days in advance.

Blueberry-Cinnamon Crumb Cake

Preparation time: 30 minutes
Baking time: 35 minutes
Makes 16 squares

Great cakes for coffee time, these
little fruity squares are also prime
candidates for dessert, served
just-warm with a splash of cream.
The batter, made with buttermilk,
is tender and light and will
accommodate just about any fruit
you want to add; turn the page for
some ideas.

For the cake

100 g soft butter, plus extra
    for greasing
150 g caster sugar
200 g plain flour
1 tsp baking powder
½ tsp bicarbonate of soda
¼ tsp salt
2 eggs, room temperature
1 tsp vanilla extract
125 g buttermilk (or use runny
    low-fat natural yoghurt)
1 tbsp milk

For the fruit layers and crumb

1 tbsp plus 1 tsp ground cinnamon
4 tbsp demerara sugar
280 g blueberries, fresh or frozen
    and defrosted
4 tbsp plain flour
a pinch of salt
30 g butter, room temperature
1 tsp icing sugar (optional)

1
Preheat the oven to 180°C (160°C fan/gas 4). Grease a 23-cm shallow square cake tin with butter, then line it with baking parchment. Put the butter and sugar in a large bowl and beat with an electric mixer until it is fluffy and light.

2
Mix the flour, baking powder, bicarbonate of soda and salt, then sift them into the bowl. Add the eggs and vanilla.

3
Beat everything together until smooth, then beat in the buttermilk or yoghurt and milk to make a smooth, creamy mixture.

4

Spoon half the batter into the prepared tin. Mix 1 tablespoon cinnamon and 2 tablespoons demerara sugar, then scatter half of this over the cake, followed by half the berries. Repeat the layers.

KEEP THEM SEPARATED
For defined layers, take care when spreading the second layer of cake batter over the blueberries, as they'll try and come along for the ride with the spatula. This will stop once you get going.

5

Make the crumb topping. Put the flour, salt, remaining cinnamon and demerara sugar in a bowl. Cut the butter into small pieces, add them to the flour, then rub together until the mixture looks like fine crumbs. When ready, squish some of the crumbs together to make big, cookie-dough-like clumps.

6

Sprinkle the crumbs over the top of the cake, then bake for 35 minutes, or until it has risen all the way to the centre, looks golden and the crumb topping is crisp. Cool in the tin for 15 minutes, then lift out the cake using the lining paper and leave to cool on a rack.

7

Dust the cake with a little icing sugar if you like, then cut it into squares to serve.

PEACH CRUMB CAKE
Replace the berries with 2 chopped ripe peaches.

APPLE & PECAN CRUMB CAKE
Thinly slice a tangy dessert apple, mix with 50 g chopped pecans, then layer as before. A few blobs of cream cheese added here and there would also make a tasty change.

Seriously Chocolatey Cookies

Preparation time: 10 minutes
Baking time: 10 minutes per batch
Makes 20

These are pure chocolate cookie heaven, with a crisp outer shell, soft middle and a bit of chewy resistance, thanks to the bittersweet treacle. They're addictive just as they are, but they also make great ice-cream sandwiches. The most important thing is not to bake them for longer than the times given.

175 g dark chocolate,
   60% cocoa solids

85 g butter

2 eggs

200 g dark brown soft sugar

1 generous tbsp black treacle

1 tsp vanilla extract

185 g plain flour

1 tbsp good-quality cocoa powder

½ tsp baking powder

¼ tsp salt

50 g dark chocolate chips
   or chopped chocolate, to stir
   through and sprinkle on top

100 g white chocolate (optional)

1
Preheat the oven to 180°C (160°C fan/gas 4) and line one or two baking trays with baking parchment. Roughly chop the chocolate and put it in a heatproof bowl with the butter, then melt until smooth.

MELTING CHOCOLATE
Place the bowl over a pan of barely simmering water (the bowl should be just larger than the rim of the pan, so that it sits happily on top), making sure it doesn't touch the water. Let the chocolate melt for about 5 minutes, stirring once or twice, until smooth throughout. Alternatively, microwave on high in 20-second bursts, stirring after each one, until smooth. It's important to use a heatproof bowl, such as Pyrex, otherwise it can become very hot and scorch the chocolate.

2
Separate one of the eggs (see page 127), then put the yolk, the whole egg, sugar, treacle and vanilla in a large bowl. Beat with a whisk or an electric mixer for about 1 minute, or until the mixture becomes smooth and a little paler.

3
Beat in the melted chocolate and butter.

4
Mix the flour, cocoa, baking powder and salt in a bowl, then sift them over the chocolate mixture. Stir together to make a soft dough, then stir in all but 1 heaped tablespoon of the chocolate chips, if using.

5

Spoon heaped tablespoons of dough onto the lined trays, leaving room for the cookies to spread. Press the remaining chocolate chips on top of the cookies. You'll find that the longer you leave the dough, the firmer it becomes, but this is fine.

6

Bake the cookies for 10 minutes for very soft centres and crisp edges (they will rise, but still feel very soft when pressed in the middle), or 12 minutes for a chewier result. Remove from the oven, let them firm up for a couple of minutes on the tray, then carefully lift onto a cooling rack and leave to cool completely.

Melt the white chocolate, if using, following the same method as before. Take extra care not to overheat it, as white chocolate will burn easily. Drizzle it over the cookies and leave to set.

7

The cookies are ready to eat as soon as the white chocolate sets, or they will keep in an airtight container for up to 3 days.

VARIATIONS
Try folding a handful of roughly chopped macadamia nuts through the dough at the same time as, or instead of, the chocolate chips. You can add milk or white chocolate chunks if you like; spices, such as ¼ teaspoon crushed cardamom seeds; raisins; or perhaps a sprinkling of crushed peppermint candy canes on top before baking for a Christmas twist. ½ teaspoon freshly ground black pepper adds warmth to the cookies, if you're making them for grown-ups. Add it with the flour (thanks to Liz, one of our photographers, for the tip).

Maple-Pecan Cinnamon Rolls

Preparation time: 40 minutes,
plus rising and proving time
Baking time: 30–35 minutes
Makes 8 large or 12 smaller rolls

Richly spiced and nutty, this version
of my favourite sticky cinnamon rolls
is just the right side of sweet, thanks
to a layer of cream cheese hidden
inside. The cardamom will bring
the wonderful scent of Scandinavian
baking to your kitchen.

For the dough

55 g butter, plus extra for greasing

150 ml milk

2 eggs

450 g strong white bread flour,
    plus extra for kneading

2 tsp fast-action yeast

50 g caster sugar

1 tsp salt

For the filling and to finish

150 g pecans

5 cardamom pods

1–2 tsp ground cinnamon,
    to your taste

2 tbsp sugar

100 ml maple syrup

250 g full-fat cream cheese,
    room temperature

1

Melt the butter in a small pan, then using a fork, beat in the milk, followed by the eggs. Sift all the dry ingredients together, then make a well in the centre.

2

Pour the wet ingredients into the dry ones, then mix with a wooden spoon to make a rough and fairly sticky dough. Leave for 5 minutes.

3

Dust the work surface with flour, then turn the dough out onto it. Start kneading, flouring the dough and your hands if you need to, but avoid adding too much. If the dough sticks a lot, scrape away any bits with a knife, wash and dry your hands and start again, dusting with more flour. After 5–10 minutes, when the dough feels very smooth and springy, put it in an oiled food storage bag or bowl, cover and leave to rise in a warm place for 1 hour, or until doubled in size.

4

Make the filling while you wait. Finely chop the pecans (or use a food processor if you have one). Bash the cardamom pods to release their seeds, discard the husks, then grind the seeds finely with a mortar and pestle. Mix the nuts, spices, sugar and 4 tablespoons of the maple syrup.

5

Flour the work surface again, then turn the risen dough out onto it. Sprinkle with a little flour, then press it out to a rectangle, about 25 x 30 cm. Spread the cream cheese all over it, going right to the edges. Scatter with the pecan mixture, then roll into a tight sausage, starting from a long edge for 12 rolls, or a short edge for 8 rolls. If it looks a bit uneven, pat the dough to straighten things up.

6
Cut the sausage into 8 or 12 slices with a large non-serrated knife dusted with flour (the flour helps stop the dough sticking).

7
Generously grease a tin with butter (a 23-cm round for 8 rolls, or a 23 x 33-cm rectangle for 12), then tuck the slices into it. Keep the seam of each spiral facing inwards. If they have squashed a bit during slicing, pat them back into shape.

8
Cover loosely with oiled clingfilm or a food storage bag, then leave to prove in a warm place for 30 minutes, or until risen. Poke the dough lightly; once ready, it will not spring back. Preheat the oven to 200°C (180°C fan/gas 6).

9
Bake for 10 minutes, then turn the oven down to 180°C (160°C fan/gas 4) and bake for another 20–25 minutes (depending on the size of your rolls), or until they have risen, are golden all over and cooked right through. If you're unsure, carefully turn the upside down out of their tin and tap sharply in the middle. It should give a hollow sound, and also be a good golden brown colour.

10
Brush the rolls with more maple syrup and enjoy the same day.

HOT CROSS BUNS OR TEACAKES
Add 2 teaspoons ground mixed spice to the flour and use 85 g sugar. Knead in 150 g dried fruit at the end of step 3 and leave to rise. Omit the filling. Shape into 12 balls, leave to prove, then slash each roll with a cross shape, brush with beaten egg and bake. Brush with a little golden syrup once out of the oven. Serve split, toasted and buttered.

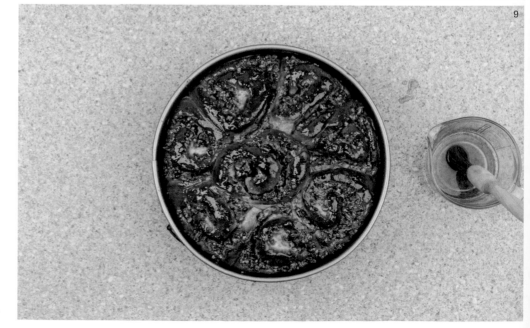

Easy Baked Doughnuts

Preparation time: 30 minutes,
plus rising and proving
Baking time: 10–12 minutes per batch
Makes 8–10 doughnuts

A very convincing doughnut is totally
possible without any deep-frying.
The secret is to make a very soft,
buttery dough that is shaped while
very cold. If cinnamon doughnuts are
your favourite, add ½ teaspoon to the
sugar. If you like them with jam, just
dunk them in. The dough can also be
glazed with beaten egg to make light
brioche-style rolls, if you prefer.

For the dough

110 g butter

180 ml milk

2 eggs

250 g plain flour, plus extra
    for dusting

1½ tsp fast-action yeast

50 g caster sugar

¼ tsp salt

oil, for greasing

For 10 sugared doughnuts

110 g butter

150 g caster sugar

For 10 glazed doughnuts

200 g icing sugar

5 tbsp milk

1 tsp vanilla extract

For 10 thickly iced doughnuts

200 g icing sugar

4 tbsp milk

1 tsp vanilla extract

a few drops of food colouring

2 tbsp sprinkles

Put the milk and butter in a small pan, then heat gently until the butter melts. Remove from the heat and leave to cool for a few minutes. Meanwhile, separate the eggs. Put the flour in a large bowl and add the yeast, sugar and salt.

SEPARATING EGGS
Gently crack the egg shell against the side of a small bowl. Slowly pull the shell apart as cleanly as possible along the crack, and pour the yolk into one half of the shell, letting the white drain into the bowl below. Pass the yolk into the other half shell to allow more white to drain away. Drop the yolk into a separate bowl. Take care not to pierce the yolk.

2

Mix the buttery milk and the yolks into the dry ingredients, to make a very wet dough, almost a batter.

3

Now comes the fun part: hold the bowl steady with one hand, then with the other, pull up as much dough as you can, then let it go, so that it slaps back into the bowl. Do this for about 5 minutes, and the dough will turn from very liquid to something with more body, and it will become stretchy and smoother. It will be much looser than ordinary bread dough, which is why this stage is all done within the safe confines of the bowl. You can do this step with a dough hook in a stand mixer, if you have one.

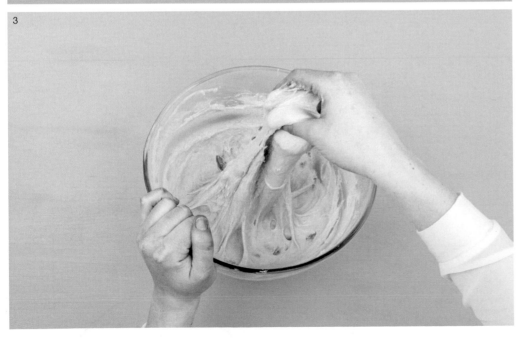

4

Oil a second bowl or a large food storage bag. Scoop the dough into it, cover the bowl with oiled clingfilm or seal the bag, then chill for at least 4 hours, or until firm. Overnight is ideal. It won't double in size like bread dough usually does.

5

Have 2 large baking trays ready, lined with baking parchment. Flour the work surface, then turn the dough out of the bowl. Dust it with flour, cut it in half and put one half in the fridge to keep cold. Shape the doughnuts in one of 3 ways, then repeat with the rest of the dough:

1) For classic ring doughnuts, roll the dough out to about 1 cm thick. Stamp the dough into circles with a 9 or 10-cm cutter, then remove the middle sections with a smaller cutter (I use my trusty egg cup). If it's your first time handling this kind of dough, I'd stick to this shape for now. Place the trimmings on top of each other, then roll again until 1 cm thick and repeat. Try not to knead the dough, as it will become springy or too warm.

2) For twists, roll the dough to a 25 x 15-cm rectangle, then cut into strips about 2.5 cm across. Pinch the ends of 2 pieces together, then twist into a rope. Pinch the other end together. Tuck the ends under to give a neat shape and pinch underneath to secure.

3) For twisted rings, proceed as for 2, but pinch the dough together in a ring shape once it has been twisted.

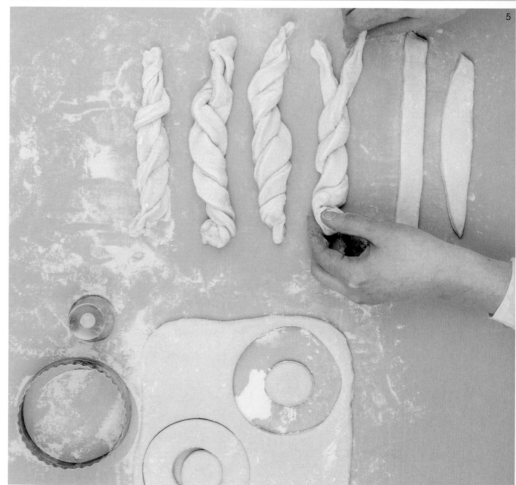

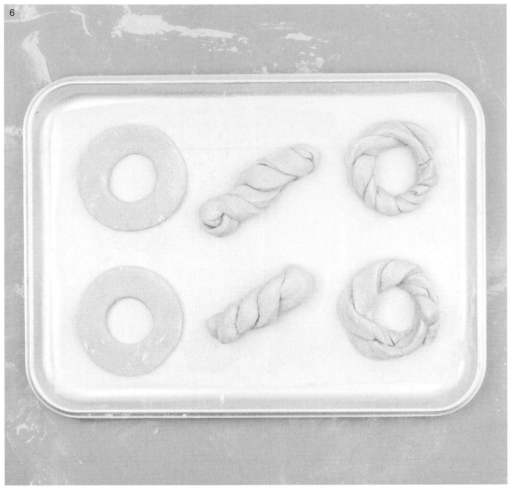

6

Lift the shapes onto a lined tray, giving the dough plenty of room to rise. Cover loosely with a tea towel or oiled clingfilm, then leave in a warm place to prove for 30 minutes–1 hour. When you see the dough is growing nicely, preheat the oven to 190°C (170°C fan/gas 5).

7

When ready to bake, the dough will have grown by about 75 per cent. If you push the side of one doughnut and your finger leaves an indent, it's ready. If not, leave them a little longer. At this point, the dough will be very delicate and difficult to move, so if they are rising unevenly, turn the tray around instead of trying to move them individually.

8

Bake for 10–12 minutes, or until dark golden and puffed up. Meanwhile, prepare your glaze, icing or sugaring ingredients. To prepare for sugared doughnuts, melt the butter in a pan, and have half the caster sugar spread out in a wide bowl. For glazed doughnuts, sift the icing sugar into a bowl, then gradually mix in the milk and vanilla, until smooth and fairly runny. For iced doughnuts, repeat as above, adding a little food colouring to make a thick paste.

9

For sugared doughnuts, turn the warm doughnuts around in the melted butter, let the excess drip away, then turn in the sugar and leave to cool. When you've sugared half the doughnuts, discard the sugar, which will be a bit buttery by now, and repeat. For glazed doughnuts, toss one doughnut at a time into the glaze, lift out with the help of 2 forks, let the excess drip away, then leave to dry on a rack. For iced doughnuts, set them on a rack, spoon the icing over them, and decorate with the sprinkles.

10

Eat the doughnuts on the day they are made. The dough can easily be made a couple of days ahead, or frozen flat on trays once shaped in step 5, then packed into freezer containers and frozen for up to 2 weeks. Spread them out on trays to thaw, then prove and bake.

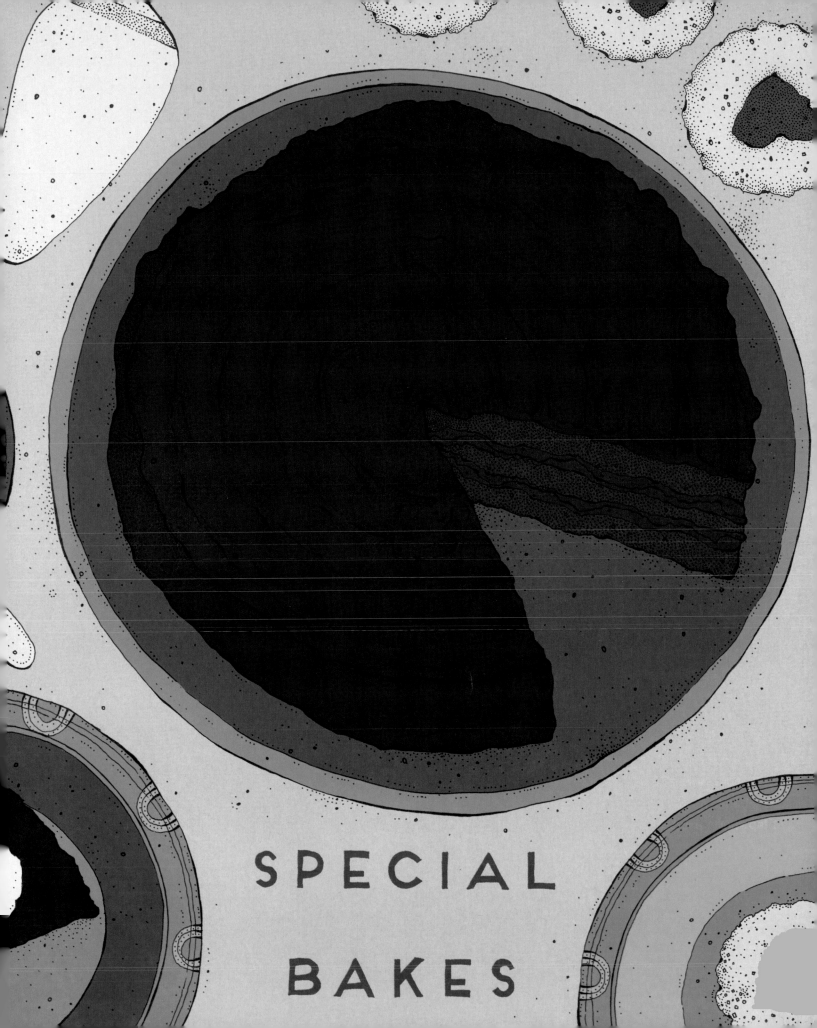

SPECIAL

BAKES

Chocolate Fudge
Layer Cake

Preparation time: 30 minutes
Baking time: 30 minutes
Makes 12 slices

If you need any persuading to make
this yummy cake, let me tell you it's
a simple stir-together method using
just two tins. The frosting is dead
easy, and the whole thing keeps
well. A go-to cake for birthdays,
Easter (with chocolate eggs on top)
or any time you need a nice piece
of good old gooey chocolate cake.

For the cake

140 g butter, plus extra for greasing

350 g plain flour

40 g cocoa powder

1 tsp bicarbonate of soda

2 tsp baking powder

¼ tsp salt

300 g light brown soft sugar

300 ml milk

150 ml vegetable oil

1 tsp vanilla extract

For the chocolate frosting

1 x 400-g can sweetened
    condensed milk

150 ml double cream

200 g dark chocolate, 50, 60 or
    70% cocoa solids, depending
    on your taste

50 g butter

1 tsp vanilla extract

1

Preheat the oven to 180°C
(160°C fan/gas 4). Put the butter
in a saucepan and melt it gently.
Meanwhile, use a little extra butter
to grease two 20-cm round sandwich
tins with removable bases, then line
the bases with baking parchment.

2

Mix together the flour, cocoa,
bicarbonate of soda, baking powder
and salt, then sift into a large bowl.

3

Add the sugar and break up any
lumps. Make a well in the centre,
pushing the mixture out to the sides
of the bowl. Whisk the milk, oil and
vanilla into the melted butter.

4

Pour the wet ingredients into the
well. Using a whisk, slowly mix
the ingredients together. Once
everything is mixed, give it a good
beating with the whisk until smooth
and evenly blended. Using a spatula,
divide the batter equally between
the tins and spread it flat.

5

Bake for 30 minutes, or until the
cakes have risen, are firm and
slightly shrunken from the sides
of the tins. Leave to cool in the tins
for 10 minutes, then turn out onto
a cooling rack and cool completely.
If you want to get ahead, wrap and
store the cakes for up to 3 days
once cooled, or freeze for up to
1 month.

6

To make the frosting, put the
condensed milk and cream in a
saucepan and stir it over a low heat
until it starts to bubble at the edges.
Take care and keep stirring, as it can
easily stick on the bottom. Break up
the chocolate into squares while you
wait, then chop it fairly small. Cut
the butter into cubes.

7

Remove the pan from the heat, add the chocolate, butter and vanilla, then leave to melt, stirring now and again. It will thicken as it cools. Beat it occasionally, until thick and fudgy and completely cooled.

8

For a four-layer cake, you'll need to cut each cake in half horizontally. You might find this easier if you chill the cake for 30 minutes beforehand.

CUTTING WITH EASE
With a large serrated knife, score a line around the 'waist' of the cake, cutting about 2.5 cm in. Turn the cake with one hand and keep the knife in the other. Keep a steady hand, and the start and finish points should meet up. Cut the cake using gentle sweeps of the knife, keeping it parallel with the surface. Rotate the cake a few degrees after each cut. You will soon reach the middle and the top half will be freed. Repeat with the second cake. If the layers end up a bit uneven after cutting, don't worry – the frosting will hide it.

9

Sandwich the cakes together on a serving plate, using about 7 tablespoons frosting between each layer. I like to put a small dot on the serving plate too, to stop the cake from moving around. Spoon the remaining frosting on top of the cake. Spread it out thickly, then, working on about a quarter of the cake at a time, work it over the edge and down to meet the plate. Try to keep going in one fluid movement. Repeat all over.

10

Smooth and swirl the frosting if you like, or leave it rough. Leave the cake to stand somewhere cool for an hour before slicing. It can be decorated the day before needed and kept in a cool, dark place.

Linzer Cookies

Preparation time: 15 minutes,
plus chilling
Baking time: 10 minutes per batch
Makes about 22

These lovely cookies are perfect
for giving at Christmas or Valentine's
– although the centres can be cut into
circles, stars or whatever shape suits
the occasion. The buttery dough is
also a versatile go-to when you need
an elegant biscuit to decorate (think
birthdays or baby showers), or as
a crisp bite to counter a creamy,
smooth dessert.

For the cookie dough

175 g soft butter, plus extra
   for greasing
85 g blanched hazelnuts
   (or use ground almonds, see Tip)
100 g caster sugar
1 egg
1 tsp vanilla extract
200 g plain flour, plus extra
   for dusting
¼ tsp salt
½ tsp ground cinnamon
1 small orange, grated zest only
   (optional)

For decorating

1 tbsp icing sugar
225 g raspberry jam (or use Nutella
   or lemon curd)

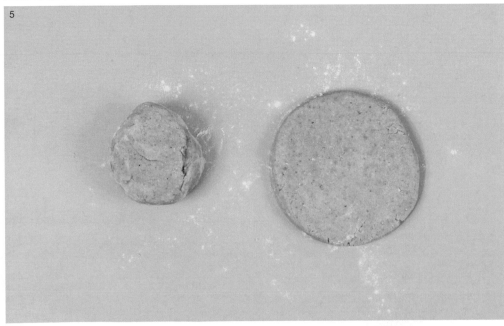

1

Preheat the oven to 180°C (160°C fan/gas 4). Lightly grease 2 baking trays with butter, then line them with baking parchment. Put the nuts in a food processor with 1 tablespoon of the sugar, then pulse until finely ground. Tip them into a bowl.

DON'T OVERDO IT
Nuts can quickly turn from finely ground to oily, clumpy and unusable. Pulsing the blades and using a little sugar should avoid this.

2

Separate the egg (see page 127), then put the yolk in the processor bowl with the remaining sugar, the vanilla and butter.

3

Process the ingredients together until creamy and evenly mixed.

4

Add the flour, salt, cinnamon and ground nuts to the processor bowl. Finely grate in the orange zest, if using, then pulse until the ingredients form a soft dough ball. You may need to scrape the sides of the bowl down once or twice.

NO PROCESSOR?
No problem: use 85 g ground almonds instead. Beat the yolk, sugar, vanilla and butter in a large bowl, using a wooden spoon or an electric mixer, until pale and creamy. Work the rest of the ingredients into the mixture using a table knife, then knead briefly to make a smooth dough.

5

Lightly dust the work surface with flour, turn out the dough onto it, then split it into 2 equal balls. Flatten each ball into a saucer-sized disc. Wrap in clingfilm and chill for 20–30 minutes, or until firm but not rock solid.

6

Sprinkle more flour on the work surface, then get ready to roll. Press ridges into one of the discs of dough with a rolling pin (this stretches it without overworking it, which makes it tough). Turn the dough and repeat this ridging a few times, until it is about 2 cm thick. If any cracks appear, pinch them together. Now roll the dough to about 3 mm thick, or about the thickness of a £1 coin.

7

Using a 6-cm fluted pastry cutter, stamp out 12 rounds. Next, using a small heart or star-shaped cutter (or the end of a wide icing tube to make a round hole), cut out shapes from the centres of half the cookies.

8

Carefully lift the whole round cookies onto one baking tray, and the cookies with the holes onto the other. Squish the remains of the dough together (taking care not to knead it, as this can make the dough tough), re-roll and stamp out more cookies until you have filled the baking trays.

9

Bake the whole cookies for 10–11 minutes and the cut-out cookies for 9 minutes, or until they are pale golden and smell nutty. Leave to stand for 2 minutes, then lift onto cooling racks and leave to cool completely. Repeat with the second batch of dough.

10

Use a fine-mesh sieve to dust the icing sugar over the cut-out cookies. Spoon about 1 teaspoon jam over the whole cookies, then sandwich together with the cut-outs. They will keep in an airtight container for 3–5 days and are best sandwiched on the day you're going to eat them.

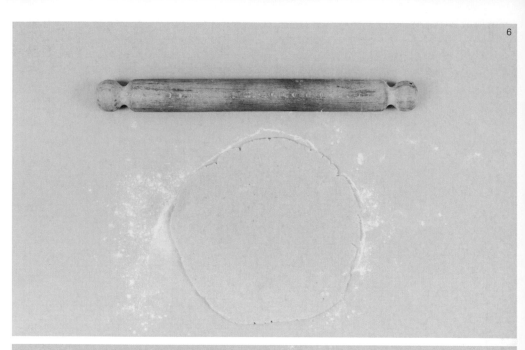

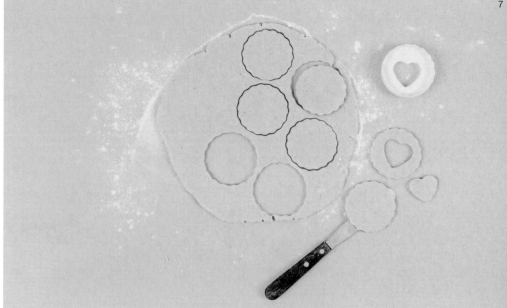

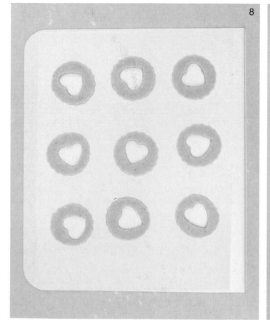

Coconut Layer Cake

Preparation time: 45 minutes
Baking time: 25 minutes
Cuts into 12 or 16 very tall pieces

Tall, frosted and a little over
the top, this cake is built from
coconut sponges alternating with
a silky-smooth coconut meringue
buttercream and lemon curd layers.
It's less sweet then a traditional
American-style frosted coconut
cake, but if you prefer it that way
see page 145 for an easy twist.

For the cake layers

50 g unsweetened desiccated
    coconut
225 g soft butter
225 g caster sugar
1 tsp vanilla extract
5 eggs, room temperature
300 g plain flour
1 tbsp baking powder
½ tsp salt
120 ml full-fat coconut milk

To decorate

5 eggs (you will only need
    the whites)
300 g icing sugar
a pinch of salt
1 tsp vanilla extract
275 g soft butter
120 ml full-fat coconut milk
300 g good-quality lemon curd
125 g toasted coconut chips

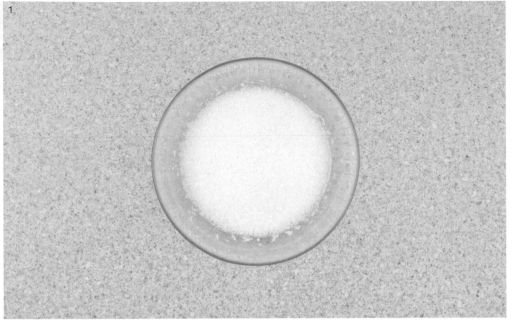

1
Soak the desiccated coconut in boiling water for 15 minutes (or longer if you can), then pour it into a sieve and press out the excess water. Use a little of the butter to grease two 20-cm round sandwich tins with removable bases, then line the bases with baking parchment. Preheat the oven to 180°C (160°C fan/gas 4).

2
Using an electric mixer, beat the butter, sugar and vanilla together until creamy and pale, scraping down the sides of the bowl every now and again with a spatula. Beat in an egg until completely combined, fluffy and light. Repeat with the other eggs, one by one. If it starts to look at all lumpy, add 1 tablespoon of the flour and it will become smooth again.

3
Thoroughly mix the flour, baking powder and salt in a bowl. Sift half into the cake batter, then fold it in using a spatula or large metal spoon. Next, fold in the coconut milk, then fold in the rest of the flour mixture, then the drained coconut.

4

Using a spatula, divide the batter evenly between the tins and spread it flat.

TAKE A SHORTCUT
If you're in a rush, the cakes can be made using the all-in-one method (see page 8), adding 1 extra teaspoon baking powder.

5

Bake for 25 minutes, or until the cakes have risen, are firm and slightly shrunken back from the sides of the tins. Leave to cool on a rack for 10 minutes, then remove from the tins and leave to cool completely.

6

For a four-layer cake, you'll need to cut each cake in half horizontally. Use a large serrated knife and score a line first around the 'waist' of the cake, then cut through gently and smoothly, rotating the cake after each cut (see page 136 for more details).

NEED MORE PRACTICE?
If your cakes are a bit uneven, don't worry, the frosting will cover it up. You could try inserting cocktail stick 'markers' into the cake at equal intervals before you start cutting. These will help you cut evenly and rebuild the cake layers in their original positions later on.

7

Clean the mixer thoroughly. For the frosting, bring 5 cm water to a simmer in a medium pan. Separate the eggs, then put the whites into a very clean, large, heatproof bowl (one that will sit just on top of the pan), and sift in the sugar. Add the pinch of salt and beat together until smooth. Sit the bowl on the pan, then beat the whites for about 7 minutes, or until very thick and shiny. It's thick enough when you can stand a teaspoon upright in the bowl without it falling over. Beat in the vanilla.

SEVEN-MINUTE FROSTING
If you prefer to use classic 7-minute frosting as a thick and fluffy cake topping, then it's ready now. It's best spread straightaway, then left to set for a while before cutting.

8

Scrape the meringue into another cold bowl, then beat for a few minutes more until just about room temperature. Keep the pan of hot water – it may come in handy in a moment. Beat the soft butter into the meringue, 1 tablespoon at a time, waiting for each one to disappear completely before adding the next. You will find that the volume of the mixture falls at first, and may seem a little loose, but keep going.

9

The frosting will suddenly change from billowy to silky and thick as you add all the butter. When all the butter has been added, gradually beat in the coconut milk. If the mixture starts to feel a bit lumpy, warm it very gently over the hot water for a few seconds while beating, and it will loosen up again.

MERINGUE BUTTERCREAM

Although more time-consuming than ordinary buttercream, meringue buttercream is a great one to have up your sleeve for a really luxurious cake frosting. It's also delicious with cooled melted dark chocolate whisked into it, instead of the coconut. Meringue buttercream is very good natured, and can be made a few days in advance, chilled, then re-beaten when ready to use. It pipes super-smoothly too.

10

You're now ready to assemble the cake. Place one layer on a serving plate and spread with half the lemon curd. Top with the second layer of cake, then add about 175 g frosting and spread it evenly to the edges. Top the third layer with the remaining lemon curd.

11

Place the final cake layer on top, then spread the remaining frosting all over the cake and smooth it with a palette knife. Mound it on the top of the cake first, then spread it down and around the cake. Press the coconut chips up the side of the cake and sprinkle them over the top.

TOASTING YOUR OWN COCONUT

Spread the coconut chips over a large, lipped baking tray. Bake at 180°C (160°C fan/gas 4) for 5 minutes, stirring halfway, until tinged with gold here and there.

12

Brush any excess chips from the serving plate. Keep the cake cool until serving. If making ahead, chill the cake, but let it come up to room temperature before eating it.

Pumpkin Pie

Preparation time: 1 hour, including
blind baking, plus chilling
Baking time: 45 minutes
Serves 12

Essential baking for autumn time
in the US, this pie is delicately set
and spiced, with a good crisp crust.
A big dollop of boozy maple cream
on the side really complements the
flavour of the pumpkin.

For the pastry

plain flour, for rolling

1 quantity sweet shortcrust
  pastry (see page 210), or use
  350 g ready-made

For the filling

3 eggs

100 g light brown soft sugar

50 g caster sugar

1 tsp vanilla extract

1½ tsp each ground cinnamon
  and ginger, mixed with ½ tsp
  ground nutmeg

120 ml double cream

120 ml milk

2 tbsp maple syrup, or 2 tbsp
  more sugar

1 x 425-g can solid-pack pumpkin
  purée (or see Tip)

a pinch of salt

For the cream

150 ml double cream

1 tbsp maple syrup

1 tbsp bourbon or whisky

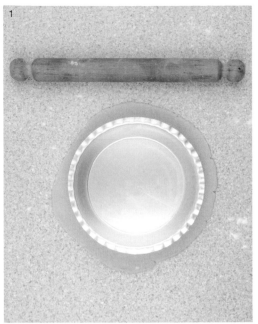

1

Lightly flour the work surface, then roll out the pastry until large enough to line a 23-cm pie tin (one with a lip is best). Use the tin as a guide for size, and try to keep the pastry as round as you can. See page 193 for full rolling instructions, if needed.

2

You can either use the rolling pin to lift the pastry into the tin, or try this method: dust the top of the pastry with a little flour, then fold it first in half, then into a triangle. Lift it into the tin, then unfold.

ANY HOLES?

Don't worry if your pastry tears before cooking, just press it back together. If cracks or holes appear after cooking, dampen a small piece of leftover pastry and smooth it over carefully.

3

Press the pastry against the edges of the dish, then trim off the overhanging pastry with a sharp knife. Prick the bottom all over with a fork, right down to the metal. Crimp the edges, if you like, pushing the pastry between your thumb and forefinger to make deep, V-shaped indents. Repeat all the way round, then chill the pastry for 15 minutes, or longer if you have time.

4

Preheat the oven to 190°C (170°C fan/gas 5). Put the tin on a baking tray. Tear a sheet of foil large enough to completely cover the pastry, edges and all. Pour in baking beans to cover the base, mounding them up a little towards the edges. Bake for 20 minutes.

5

Check under the foil; if the pastry looks dry and set, remove the covering. If not, bake for another 5 minutes. When ready, carefully spoon out the hot baking beans, then remove the paper or foil. Bake for another 15–20 minutes, or until it is golden and feels sandy. If the edges colour before the base is ready, cover them with foil.

6

Make the filling while you wait. Beat the eggs, saving 1 tablespoon to glaze the pastry case later. Beat the rest of the filling ingredients into the eggs, to make a thin custard.

HOME-MADE PUMPKIN PURÉE
To make your own purée, roast large chunks of pumpkin with just a little oil for 30 minutes at 200°C (180°C fan/gas 6), or until softened, or microwave them. Purée or mash well, then pass through a sieve until smooth. Add 425 g to the rest of the filling ingredients once cooled.

7

Now we need to seal the pastry, as the filling is so liquid. Brush the pastry all over with 1 tablespoon reserved beaten egg, then bake for 2 more minutes, until shiny.

8

Pull the oven rack out a little. Pour the filling into the crust, without letting it overflow, and slide the oven rack back in.

9

Bake for 45 minutes, or until the edges have risen slightly and the centre wobbles gently. Leave to cool in the tin. To make the cream, whip the ingredients together until just thickened.

10

Serve the pie at room temperature or chilled, with the cream.

Angel Cake with Berries

Preparation time: 30 minutes
Baking time: 35 minutes
Makes at least 12 slices

Angel food cake is like no other:
a soft, cloud-like sponge made
without yolks or fat, and not as
tricky as you might think. I like
serving it for dessert with a light,
creamy topping and seasonal fruit
to balance the sweetness, but you
can also use the cake recipe as
a base and get creative with one
of the other frostings in the book.

For the cake

1 vanilla pod or 1 tsp vanilla paste

1 orange

115 g plain flour

1 tbsp cornflour

50 g icing sugar

½ tsp salt

10 eggs (whites only), at room
   temperature

1 tsp cream of tartar

300 g caster sugar

For the topping

150 g thick Greek yoghurt

250 ml double cream

3–4 tbsp icing sugar, or to taste

fresh summer berries and cherries,
   plus raspberry coulis, if you like
   (see page 154)

1

Preheat the oven to 180°C (160°C fan/gas 4). Split the vanilla pod lengthways and scrape out the seeds with the tip of the knife. Grate the zest from the orange, reserving the fruit for later. Mix the flour, cornflour, icing sugar and salt, then sift together twice to make sure they are completely evenly mixed and lump-free.

2

Separate the eggs (see page 127), then put the whites in a large, scrupulously clean bowl with the cream of tartar. Using an electric mixer, whisk the whites until frothy and light. You won't need the yolks, but you could use them to make the lemon curd recipe on page 192.

WHICH BOWL FOR WHISKING?
A metal or ceramic bowl is best for whipping meringue mixtures – plastic bowls can hide little bits of grease in scratches, and grease is the enemy of fluffy egg whites.

3

Add the vanilla seeds and orange zest and keep whisking until the mixture holds itself in stiff peaks. The key is to stop beating before the meringue starts to look dry or separated at the edges.

4

Add 1 tablespoon of the caster sugar, then beat again until the mixture returns to stiff peaks. Repeat this until all the sugar has been incorporated, and the meringue is thick and shimmery, like shaving foam.

5

Sift the flour mixture over the meringue. Using a large metal spoon, fold it in until combined and smooth, cutting and lifting the flour through the foam rather than stirring, to preserve the air bubbles.

6

Using a spatula, scrape the batter into a 25-cm angel cake tin and level the top. The tin isn't greased or lined, as the cake needs to be able to 'grip' and rise up the sides of the tin as it bakes.

7

Bake for 35 minutes, or until the cake is golden and has risen well. It's ready when a skewer inserted into the centre comes out clean. Angel cakes need to be cooled upside-down. If your tin has feet, turn it over and leave to cool. If not, turn it upside down on a cooling rack or invert it onto a bottle, or something that will keep the top of the cake exposed to the air as it cools. Don't worry, it won't fall out. When the cake has cooled, carefully sweep a palette knife around the tin to loosen it, then push the base of the tin up to expose the cake. You may need to ease the centre of the tin away from the cake too.

8

Transfer the cake to a serving plate. To make the topping, squeeze 2 tablespoons juice from the orange and combine it with the yoghurt, cream and icing sugar. Beat until smooth and thick. Taste and add more sugar, if you like. When ready to serve, smooth the topping over the cake either in a thick layer on top, or a thinner layer all over.

9

Serve with the berries and a little coulis, if you like.

TO MAKE YOUR OWN COULIS
Process or mash 450 g fresh or frozen raspberries with 2 tablespoons icing sugar until as smooth as possible, then strain out the pips. Taste and add more sugar if needed.

Sticky Pear & Pecan Toffee Cake

Preparation time: 20 minutes
Baking time: 50 minutes
Cuts into 12 slices

Many bakers have dreams of opening a little café with cakes on the counter and really good coffee. In mine, I'd be making this every day in autumn, using plums, apples or cranberries closer to the holidays. It's here in this chapter because I can imagine it crowning the table at Christmas, too.

For the cake
150 g soft pitted dates
225 g soft butter, plus extra
    for greasing
150 g pecans
2 medium, just-ripe pears
200 g light brown soft sugar
4 eggs, room temperature
4 tbsp milk
300 g plain flour
1 tsp bicarbonate of soda
1 tsp baking powder
2 tsp ground cinnamon or
    ground mixed spice
¼ tsp salt

For the toffee topping
100 g light brown soft sugar
2 tbsp butter
100 ml double cream
50 g pecans

1
First, soak the dates by covering them with boiling water. Leave to stand for 15 minutes, or longer if you like. Meanwhile, preheat the oven to 160°C (140°C fan/gas 3) and do the rest of the prep. Melt a little butter, then use a pastry brush to grease the inside of a 25-cm non-stick bundt tin.

NO BUNDT TIN?
Using a bundt tin gives this cake a wonderful texture and dramatic shape, but a greased and lined 23 x 33-cm traybake tin does the job too. Bake the cake at 160°C (140°C fan/gas 3) for 40 minutes, or until it has risen right to the middle, and a skewer inserted into the centre comes out clean.

2
Finely chop the pecans in a food processor, then tip them out. Peel the pears, then cut them into fingertip-sized chunks, discarding the central core part.

3
Drain the dates through a sieve. Process the butter and sugar together until creamy and smooth, then whizz in the dates. Now add the eggs, milk, flour, bicarbonate of soda, baking powder, cinnamon and salt and process to make a smooth cake batter.

MAKING IT BY HAND
This recipe is much easier with a food processor, but you can make it by hand too. Finely chop the nuts, and chop the soaked dates as finely as you can, almost to a pulp. Mix the dates and other ingredients in a large bowl and beat until creamy and smooth. Fold in the nuts and pears and continue.

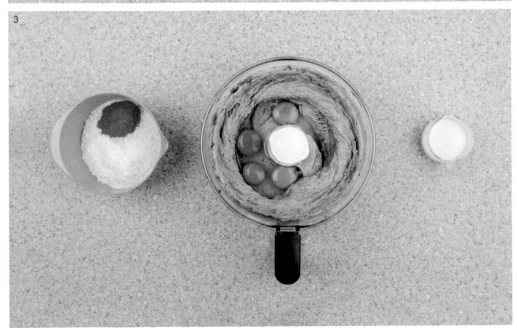

4

Unless you have a really big food processor, at this point you'll need to turn the batter into a bowl to fold in the pecans and pears. If you do have the room in the processor bowl, be sure to remove the blades before mixing. Spoon the batter into the prepared tin and smooth the top.

5

Bake for 50 minutes, or until the cake has risen all over and a skewer inserted into the centre comes out clean. Let the cake cool in the tin for at least 10 minutes before giving the tin a sharp tap on the work surface, then turning it out onto a cooling rack if serving cold, or a plate if serving warm.

6

For the toffee topping, put the sugar, butter and cream in a medium pan. Heat it gently until the sugar has dissolved, then simmer briefly to make a silky smooth caramel sauce.

7

Stir the pecans into the sauce, then spoon it all over the cake. It will set firm and lose its shine if serving cold, but it will be easier to slice.

8

The cake will keep in an airtight container for up to 3 days, and will freeze well, without the topping.

TRY THIS
Make a double quantity of the toffee sauce, and serve the sauce and the cake warm, at the table, as a spectacular dessert. Great with cream or crème anglaise served alongside.

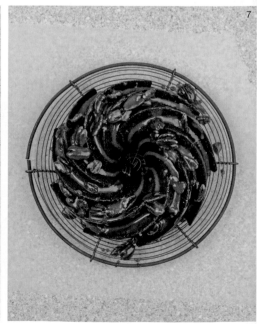

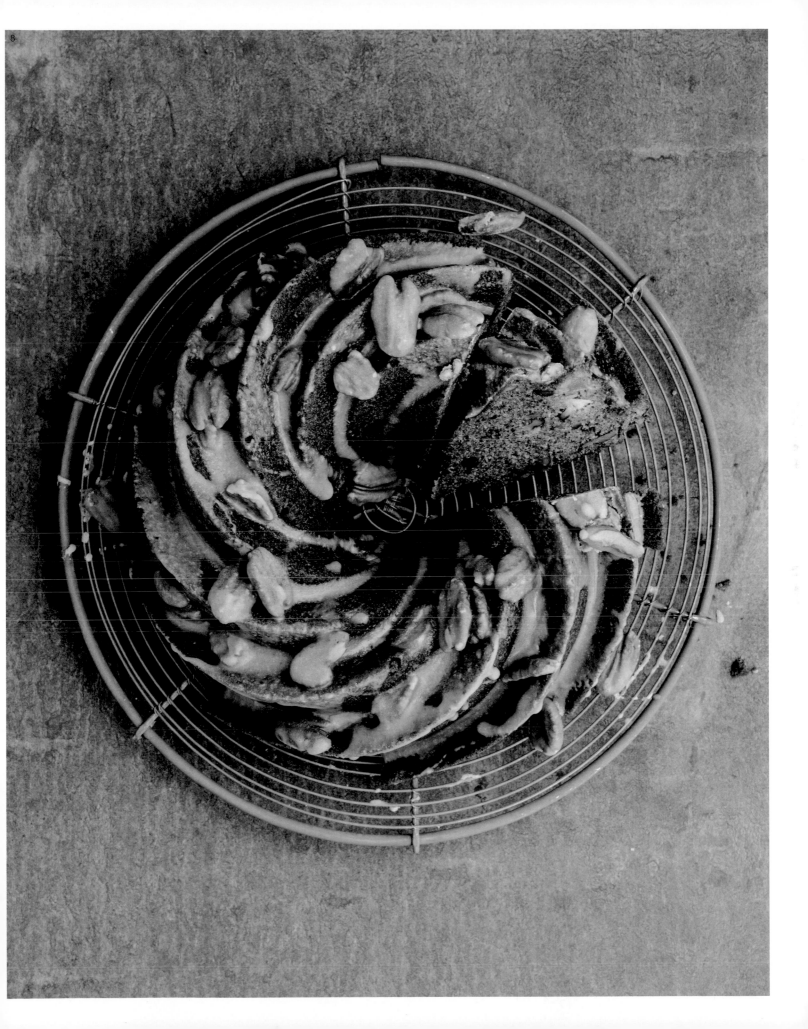

Frosted Cupcakes

Preparation time: 25 minutes
Baking time: 18–20 minutes
Makes 12 cupcakes

When I teach baking, the thing most students seem to want to master is a good piped cupcake. It does take practice, but you'll soon be swirling frosting like a pro. Here, the classic recipe gets an upgrade with a white chocolate frosting that is easy to flavour, colour and pipe. Too fancy? Use the ordinary buttercream on page 46 and double it.

For the cupcakes

175 g butter

150 g buttermilk or runny low-fat
   plain yoghurt

4 eggs

1 tsp vanilla paste or extract

150 g plain flour

2 tsp baking powder

¼ tsp salt

175 g caster sugar

100 g ground almonds

For the white chocolate frosting

120 ml double cream

100 g white chocolate

175 g soft butter

½ tsp vanilla paste or extract

a pinch of salt

250 g icing sugar

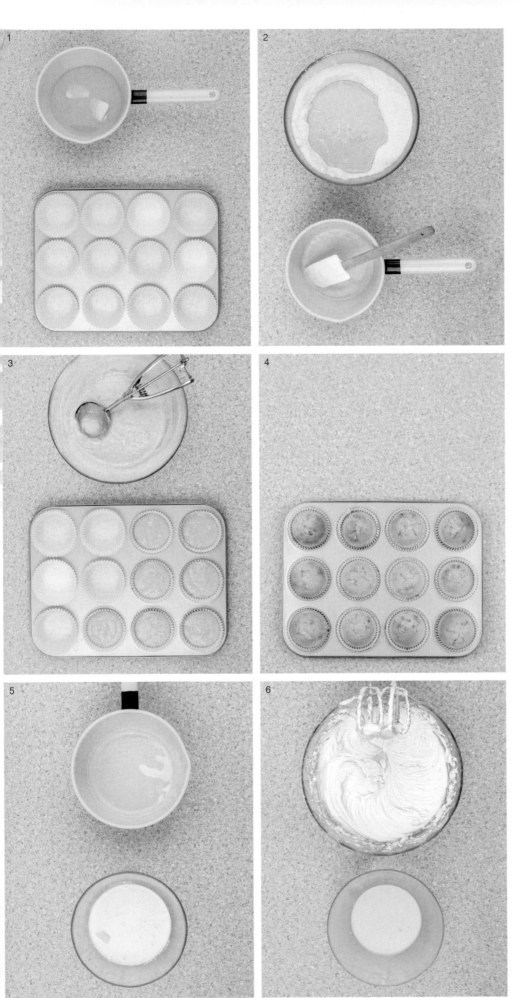

1

Line a 12-hole muffin tin with deep paper cases. Preheat the oven to 190°C (170°C fan/gas 5). Melt the butter in a pan, remove from the heat and leave to cool a little. Stir the buttermilk into the butter, then add the eggs and vanilla. Beat together with a fork until smooth.

2

Mix together the flour, baking powder and salt, then sift into a large bowl. Stir in the sugar and almonds. Make a well in the centre, then pour in the butter mixture.

3

Using a spatula or balloon whisk, quickly mix together until smooth and lump-free. Fill the cases using an ice cream scoop, or hold the bowl over the tin while you spoon it in. The cases should be quite full.

4

Bake for 18–20 minutes, or until they have risen evenly, are golden brown and smell sweet. A skewer inserted into one of the middle cupcakes; it should come out clean. Cool for 5 minutes, then transfer to a rack and cool completely.

5

To make the frosting, put the cream in a small pan and heat until the edges are just starting to bubble. Meanwhile, roughly chop the chocolate and put it in a small bowl. Pour the hot cream over the chocolate, then let it melt, stirring occasionally. Leave to cool.

6

Put the butter in a large bowl, beat well until creamy, add the vanilla and salt, then gradually beat in the icing sugar until fluffy and pale. Gradually pour in the cooled chocolate, then beat to make a very light, smooth frosting. Work in more sugar if it seems too soft.

7

To frost with a palette knife, mound 2 tablespoons frosting onto the cake. For neatly sloped sides, turn the cupcake clockwise in one hand while smoothing anti-clockwise with the other, holding the blade at a slight angle. Dip the knife into the frosting on top, turning it as before, to make an indent with a tall ridge around it. Clean the knife against the edge of the bowl before each stage.

8

To pipe roses, cut the first 2.5 cm or so from a disposable piping bag, insert a 2D rose nozzle, then spoon in the frosting. Don't fill it more than half full. Twist the bag at the top to create pressure behind the tip. Start in the middle of the cake, then pipe outwards in a spiral. Pipe as evenly as you can, keeping the bag upright. If you go wrong, scrape the frosting back into the bowl (avoiding crumbs) and try again. Twist the top of the bag to increase the pressure before piping each cake.

CHOCOLATE OREO CUPCAKES
Use 125 g flour and 3 tablespoons cocoa powder in the batter. Make the frosting with dark chocolate instead of white, or crush Oreos into the white frosting. Top with half a cookie.

PEANUT BUTTER CUPCAKES
Replace 3 tablespoons butter with smooth peanut butter in the basic batter. For the frosting, replace the chocolate and cream with 175 g smooth peanut butter. Top with Reese's Pieces.

PISTACHIO CUPCAKES
Grind 150 g shelled pistachios in a processor and add 100 g to the batter instead of the almonds. Colour the frosting very pale green. Frost the cakes, then sprinkle with the rest of the pistachios.

Red Velvet Whoopie Pies

Preparation time: 20 minutes
Baking time: 10 minutes per batch
Makes 24 complete pies

If you feel like a change from cupcakes, whoopie pies are the answer. These attention-grabbing cakes are fun to make for Halloween or Valentine's. Unlike a classic whoopie, these are soft and delicate, like their namesake red velvet cake. Leave out the food colouring if you prefer, for a pale, chocolatey look.

For the batter

175 g soft butter, plus extra
   for greasing
200 g caster sugar
1 tsp vanilla pod paste or extract
250 g plain flour
25 g cocoa powder
1½ tsp bicarbonate of soda
½ tsp baking powder
¼ tsp salt
3 eggs
125 g buttermilk
1 tsp red food colouring paste

For the filling and decoration

175 g soft butter
400 g full-fat cream cheese, cold
1 tsp vanilla paste or extract
150 g icing sugar
50 g white chocolate

1
Preheat the oven to 180°C (160°C fan/gas 4). Lightly grease and line 2 baking trays with baking parchment. Put the butter, sugar and vanilla in a large bowl and beat with an electric mixer or a wooden spoon until creamy and light.

2
Mix together the flour, cocoa, bicarbonate of soda, baking powder and salt, then sift them into a bowl. Put the eggs, buttermilk and food colouring in the bowl with the butter and sugar.

3
Sift the flour mixture into the bowl, then beat to a smooth, bright-red batter. It will be quite thick and sticky.

4
Spoon the mixture evenly onto the lined baking trays, aiming for 48 balls, about 1 heaped teaspoon each. Leave room for the batter to spread a bit as it cooks. I use a small cookie scoop to get a nicely uniform round shape, but you can push the batter off the end of a spoon with your finger, or pipe it instead. You'll need to bake them in several batches.

5
Bake the whoopies for 9–10 minutes, or until they have risen and are firm to the touch, but not crisp. Leave to cool for a few minutes on the trays, then remove to a cooling rack and cool completely.

6

To make the filling, put the butter in a large bowl and beat with an electric mixer until very creamy and smooth. Add the cream cheese and vanilla and beat briefly until evenly blended. Now sift in the icing sugar and beat for a few seconds more until smooth and creamy, or work it in gently with a spatula. If your kitchen is warm, chill the frosting while the whoopies cool.

7

Once cool, spread or pipe a generous amount of filling onto the flat sides of half the cakes, then top with the remaining halves and squeeze together gently so that the frosting shows at the sides.

8

Finely grate the white chocolate, then roll the edges of the whoopies in it to coat. It will stick to the filling.

9

Eat the whoopies the day they are made, or soon after. Keep them in the fridge, but eat them at room temperature. If you are not filling them straightaway, pack them carefully with baking parchment between the layers.

BANOFFEE WHOOPIE PIES
Beat 1 mashed ripe banana into the creamed butter and sugar. Use 2 eggs and 280 g flour and omit the cocoa. Sandwich with the filling plus 1 heaped teaspoon dulce de leche, then roll the edges in grated dark chocolate.

PUMPKIN PIE WHOOPIE PIES
Use 250 g light brown soft sugar. Beat 250 g pumpkin purée into the creamed butter and sugar. Use 2 eggs, 280 g flour (omit the cocoa) and add 1 tablespoon ground mixed spice. Flavour the filling with the grated zest of 1 orange.

Vanilla Celebration Cake

Preparation time: about 1 hour
15 minutes
Baking time: 1 hour 30–40 minutes
Serves 20, or more (see page 10)

I'm often asked to make cakes
for weddings, anniversaries
and birthdays, so I understand
the pressure you might feel if
you've been asked the same thing.
You need a reliable recipe that keeps
well, cuts cleanly, tastes good and
looks fabulous. This recipe, with its
luxurious white chocolate frosting,
should do it.

For the cake
350 g soft butter, plus extra
   for greasing
6 eggs, room temperature
350 g caster sugar
1 tsp vanilla paste
385 g plain flour
1 tbsp plus 1 tsp baking powder
4 tbsp cornflour
½ tsp salt
300 g buttermilk

For the syrup
50 g sugar
½ tsp vanilla paste

For the frosting
350 ml double cream
175 g white chocolate
350 g soft butter
1 tsp vanilla paste
¼ tsp salt
650 g icing sugar, or more if needed

1
Preheat the oven to 160°C (140°C fan/gas 3). Double-line a 23-cm springform or ordinary 23-cm deep round cake tin (see page 177). Separate 3 of the eggs and add the whites to 3 whole eggs. (You won't need the yolks here.)

2
Using an electric mixer, beat the butter, sugar and vanilla together until very creamy and pale. Pour a little of the egg into the bowl, then beat in until fluffy and light. Repeat until all the egg has been used. If the batter starts to look a little lumpy at any point, beat in 1 tablespoon of the flour.

3
Mix the flour, baking powder, cornflour and salt together in a bowl. Sift half of this into the cake batter, fold it in, then fold in the buttermilk. Follow with the rest of the flour mixture to make a smooth and fairly thick batter.

4
Spoon the batter into the tin and level the top. Make a slight dip in the centre, which will encourage the cake to rise without a dome.

5
Bake for 1 hour 30–40 minutes, or until it has risen well and is golden, and a skewer inserted into the centre comes out clean. Check carefully, as the cake may sink or seem heavy if underdone. In the meantime, make the syrup: gently heat the sugar, 3 tablespoons water and vanilla until the sugar dissolves. Set aside. Once out of the oven, let the cake cool in the tin until just warm, then poke 25 holes right through it. Slowly spoon the syrup over it, letting it soak in after each addition. Leave to cool completely in the tin. It can be wrapped and frozen for up to 1 month.

6

For the frosting, put the cream in a small pan and heat until the edges are just starting to bubble. Chop the chocolate into small pieces and put in a small heatproof bowl. Pour the hot cream over it, then let it melt, stirring now and again, until smooth and silky. Leave to cool completely.

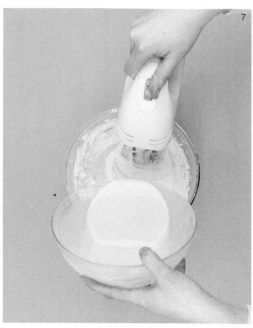

7

Put the butter, vanilla and salt in a large bowl, beat well until smooth and creamy, then slowly beat in the icing sugar to make a fluffy buttercream. Gradually pour in the cooled white chocolate and beat to make a very pale, silky-smooth frosting. If it seems too soft, add a little more sugar.

8

Split the cake horizontally into 3 even layers using a large serrated knife (see page 136). Stack it back together, spreading about 200 g frosting between each layer.

9

Now we're going to cover the cake in a 'crumb coat', which gives it a perfect finish. Mound 250 g of the frosting onto the cake, then spread it over the top and down the sides to meet the plate. Try not to lift the palette knife off the cake, but move it in a fluid movement. Smooth, then chill for 10 minutes, or until firm.

10

Spread the remaining frosting over the cake as before. If this all sounds too tricky, leave the frosting ruffled and rustic. Store in a cool place (or the fridge if it's a hot day) to let the frosting set a little. It can be wrapped and chilled for up to 2 days; allow to come to room temperature before eating. To top with flowers, tie together your favourite blooms, wrap the ends in clingfilm, then sit them on top of, or to the side of, the finished cake.

Chocolate Hazelnut Log

Preparation time: 35 minutes,
plus chilling
Baking time: 15 minutes
Serves 8–10

This variation on a classic Yule log
is a perfect Christmas treat that kids
will love to help with. But don't just
save it for December; when scored
and rolled from one of the narrow
ends, it makes a fat, swirly roulade
for a special dessert at any time of
year. Use 70% dark chocolate and
serve it with berries.

For the cake

a little butter, for greasing

6 eggs, room temperature

150 g light brown soft sugar

1 tbsp plain flour

a pinch of salt

50 g good-quality cocoa powder,
    plus 2 tbsp for rolling

For the filling

200 g dark chocolate,
    60% cocoa solids

600 ml double cream

200 g Nutella

1 tsp vanilla extract

icing sugar, to dust

1

Grease the base and sides of a
25 x 37-cm Swiss roll tin or rimmed
baking tray, then line the base with
baking parchment. Preheat the oven
to 180°C (160°C fan/gas 4). Put the
eggs and the sugar in a large bowl
and whisk with an electric mixer at
medium speed until thick, mousse-
like and doubled in volume. It will
take 5 minutes or so.

2

Mix the flour, salt and cocoa in
a bowl, then sift them over the
whisked eggs. Fold them in using
a large metal spoon or spatula,
cutting and lifting rather than
stirring. This will preserve the air
bubbles trapped inside the batter.
It might take longer than you expect
to get the batter to an almost
even brown.

3

Holding the bowl just above
the prepared baking tin (pouring
from a great height will knock
the bubbles flat), pour in the cake
batter. Tilt the tin slowly from side
to side, letting the batter run into
the corners.

4

Bake for 15 minutes, or until the
cake has risen all over and the sides
are shrinking away from the edge
of the tin. It's best to loosen the
cake away from the tin carefully
with a palette knife now, in case
it has stuck a little.

5

Spread a large sheet of baking
parchment on the work surface,
then sift the 2 tablespoons cocoa
powder over it. Flip the cake onto
this sheet, remove the tin, then
cover the cake with a clean tea
towel and leave to cool. The cloth
will trap steam as the cake cools,
helping it stay soft and moist.

6
Make the filling. Chop the chocolate into small pieces. Heat 300 ml of the cream in a pan until it bubbles at the edges. Take off the heat and stir in the chocolate, Nutella and vanilla. Let it melt to make a smooth ganache, then set aside until it has cooled, but is still fairly liquid.

7
Pour the rest of the cream into a bowl, add about 150 g of the chocolate ganache, then whisk until very thick, but not stiff.

8
When the cake has cooled, remove the tea towel, then carefully peel off the baking parchment. Trim about 1 cm from each edge with a serrated knife. Score a line in the cake about 2.5 cm in from the nearest long end.

9
Spread the filling over the cake, then roll it up from the scored end. Use the paper to help make a tight roll.

10
Roll the cake onto a clean piece of baking parchment. Cut about 10 cm from one end, at an angle.

11
Transfer the large piece to a serving plate, then nestle the shorter one against it to make a branch. Spread the remaining ganache all over, adding plenty of texture with the knife. Chill for at least 1 hour, or up to 3 days.

12
Remove from the fridge 30 minutes before eating and dust with icing sugar to serve.

Festive Fruit Cake

Preparation time: 30 minutes, plus
soaking and optional feeding time
Baking time: 2¾–3 hours
Makes about 24 slices

It's not Christmas for me without
a home-made fruit cake, but I'm
always keen for it to be fruity and
light rather than too heavy or rich.
This one can be eaten straightaway,
or matured, it's up to you. You can
change the dried fruit to what suits
you, plus the decorating is optional –
see the tips on pages 177 and 180.

For the cake

1 lemon

100 g glacé cherries, drained

600 g dried mixed fruit, such as
   raisins, sultanas or currants

100 g candied mixed citrus peel

120 ml brandy or dark rum (see Tip)

225 g soft butter, plus extra
   for greasing

225 g light brown soft sugar

1 tsp vanilla extract

4 eggs

225 g plain flour

2 tsp ground mixed spice

¼ tsp salt

50 g toasted flaked almonds

To decorate

2 tbsp apricot jam, marmalade
   or cake glaze

icing sugar, for dusting

500 g ready-made marzipan

500 g ready-to-roll fondant icing

edible glitter and ribbon (optional),
   or decorations of your choice

1

Finely grate the zest from the lemon and squeeze the juice. Cut the cherries in half. Put them into a large saucepan with the dried fruit and peel and 100 ml of the alcohol. Cover, then bring to a simmer. Remove from the heat and leave to stand for at least 1 hour, or overnight if you can. The fruit will plump up and absorb the liquid.

SOAKING ALTERNATIVES
If you'd rather not use alcohol, strong black tea makes a good substitute, as does orange or apple juice. Alcohol is added to act as a flavouring, as well as to preserve the cake until Christmas. Any dried fruit can be substituted, although I'd recommend a balance of sweet and tart fruit for a more interesting end result.

2

When ready to make the cake, preheat the oven to 160°C (140°C fan/gas 3). Double-line a deep 20-cm round cake tin with baking parchment. To do this, fold a 65 x 30-cm piece of parchment in half lengthways. On the folded side, make a fold about 2 cm of the way in. Snip at 2-cm intervals along the length of the seam, up to the fold, to make a frill. Cut 2 circles for the base.

3

Grease the tin with butter, then line the sides with the frilled paper, with the frills at the base of the tin, overlapping slightly. Grease the circles with butter, then sit them on top, trapping the frill below. This preparation is needed to protect the cake during the long baking time.

4

Put the butter and sugar in a large bowl, then beat with an electric mixer until pale and creamy. Add the vanilla, then beat in 1 egg. When the mixture is fluffy and light, add the next egg and repeat. If the batter starts to look a little lumpy, beat in 1 tablespoon of the flour. Repeat with the remaining eggs. This is one creaming-method cake that can't be sped up; don't try to make it using the all-in-one method.

5

Sift the flour, spice and salt into the bowl and fold into the batter with a spatula or large metal spoon. Now fold in the soaked fruit, plus the nuts. It will make a stiff batter.

6

Scrape the batter into the prepared tin and level the top. Make a depression in the middle of the batter with the spatula. This will help the cake rise more evenly.

7

Bake for 1½ hours, then turn the oven down to 150°C (130°C fan/gas 2) for 1¼–1½ hours more. When ready, the cake will be dark golden, and a skewer inserted into the centre will come out clean. If not, bake for another 15 minutes and check again. Leave to cool in its tin on a rack. When still warm, prick holes all over it with a cocktail stick and spoon in the rest of the alcohol, tea or juice. Once cool, remove from the tin, then wrap carefully in clean baking parchment and store in an airtight container in a cool place.

FEEDING YOUR CAKE
This cake is perfectly good when eaten as soon as it's cooled, but it can be matured over a couple of months. Spoon 1 tablespoon of your chosen soaking liquid over it 3 times before Christmas, allowing at least 1 week between each feeding. Wrap and store carefully each time to prevent the cake from drying out.

8

When ready to decorate, choose a cake plate or board that's a little larger than the cake itself. Melt the jam, marmalade or cake glaze with 1 teaspoon water, then push it through a sieve to remove any lumps. Brush the strained jam over the top of the cake. This will be the glue for the marzipan.

9

Dust the work surface generously with icing sugar. Knead the marzipan a few times to soften it a little, then shape it into a ball. Roll with a rolling pin, turning the marzipan by 90 degrees with every few rolls, until it is a circle about the same size as the cake. Use your hands to help shape the circle if it's a little uneven. Put it on the cake.

ICING ALTERNATIVES

Half-covering the cake is a great way to try your hand at icing without the challenge of covering a cake entirely. Or, if you'd rather avoid cake decorating all together, why not press whole shelled almonds into the top of the cake instead, before baking? When ready to serve, brush with the glaze or dust with icing sugar and fix a ribbon around it.

10

Making sure there are no lumps of marzipan on the work surface, repeat the process using two thirds of the fondant icing, shaping it with your hands if you need to. Roll the rest of the icing to about 3 mm thick, then cut out festive shapes with a cookie cutter.

11

Bring some water to the boil and let it cool a little. Dampen a clean pastry brush in the boiled water and, sparingly but evenly, brush it over the marzipan. Lay the fondant on top of the marzipan, then stick the cut-out shapes on top, again using a little water as glue. Sprinkle with edible glitter, if using, and tie a ribbon around the cake.

12

Leave the fondant to dry for a few hours, then store in an airtight container until needed.

NOT QUITE STRAIGHT?

If the circle of marzipan or fondant is too big once it's on the cake, don't worry. If it's too big, gently rub a tall, straight-sided glass around the edge of the cake, which will press the fondant and marzipan in and level things up. If the circle is too small, rub it with the flat of your hand to press it outwards a little.

Cranberry Stollen

Preparation time: 45 minutes,
plus rising and proving
Baking time: 30 minutes
Makes 2 family-size loaves

Several wintry trips to Germany have
given me a real fondness for stollen,
the richly fruited Christmas loaf
with the hidden treasure of marzipan
inside. The recipe makes two loaves;
eat one straight after baking, then
wrap the other one well and stash
it in the freezer for up to 1 month.

For the bread

1 lemon

4 tbsp dark rum (or use orange juice)

1 tsp vanilla extract

150 g dried cranberries

150 g sultanas (or use chopped
    dried apricots)

300 ml milk

1 tbsp fast-action yeast

1 whole nutmeg, or use 1 tsp ground

500 g strong white bread flour, plus
    extra for dusting

1 tsp salt

85 g sugar

175 g butter, room temperature

2 eggs

250 g marzipan

To finish

50 g butter

25 g icing sugar

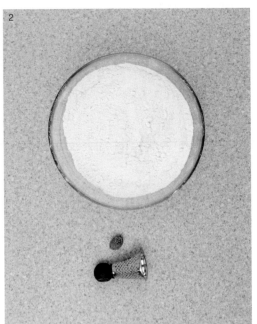

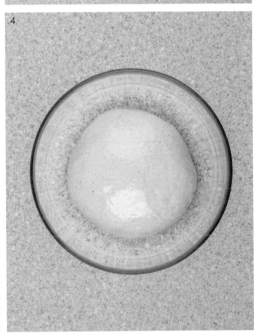

1

Finely grate the lemon zest and mix it with the rum or orange juice, vanilla and dried fruit. Let macerate while you make the dough. Gently warm the milk in the microwave or in a pan, then whisk in the yeast. The milk must only be warm; if it's too hot, it will kill the yeast.

2

If using whole nutmeg, grate 2 teaspoons. Sift the flour into a large bowl with the salt, then add the nutmeg and sugar. Cut the butter into cubes, then rub it into the flour mixture using your fingertips, until the mixture looks like breadcrumbs.

3

Separate one of the eggs (see page 127). Add the yolk and whole egg to the milk and beat together. Using a wooden spoon, mix the liquid into the rubbed-in mixture to make a soft, sticky dough. Leave to stand for 10 minutes.

4

Dust the work surface with flour, then turn the dough out onto it. Flour the top of the dough and your hands, then begin to knead (see page 69 for guidance). Keep going for about 10 minutes, until the dough feels very springy or elastic and silky smooth. Use more flour if you need to. Put the dough in an oiled bowl and cover with oiled clingfilm.

5

Leave to rise in a warm place for 1½ hours, or until doubled in size.

6

Turn the dough out onto the floured work surface and cut it in half. Use your hands to press and pat each half into an 20 x 40-cm rectangle. Spread the soaked fruit over the bottom half of each one, then fold the top half over it.

7

Pat the dough out to about 15 x 25 cm, then fold it in half again along the long edge; repeat this twice, or until the fruit is well distributed in the dough, but isn't escaping. You should end up with 2 rectangles about 15 x 25 cm. If at any point the dough starts being too springy to handle, leave it to sit for a few minutes, then continue.

8

Roll the marzipan into 2 equal sausages. Make a deep groove along the length of each piece of dough, then place the marzipan in it.

9

Roll one side of the dough over the marzipan. Press and pinch the edges together well to make a lip of dough, then shape the ends of the loaves into slight points.

10

Line a large baking tray with baking parchment and lift the breads onto it. Leave room for rising. Cover with oiled clingfilm and leave to prove in a warm place for 1 hour, or until almost doubled in size. Preheat the oven to 180°C (160°C fan/gas 4).

11

Bake for 30 minutes, or until the breads have risen well and are dark golden brown. Melt the butter, then brush it all over the warm stollen and dredge with icing sugar.

12

Leave to cool completely before wrapping and storing. Dust with icing sugar again before bringing it to the table.

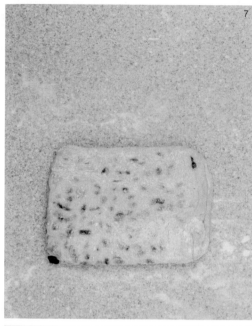

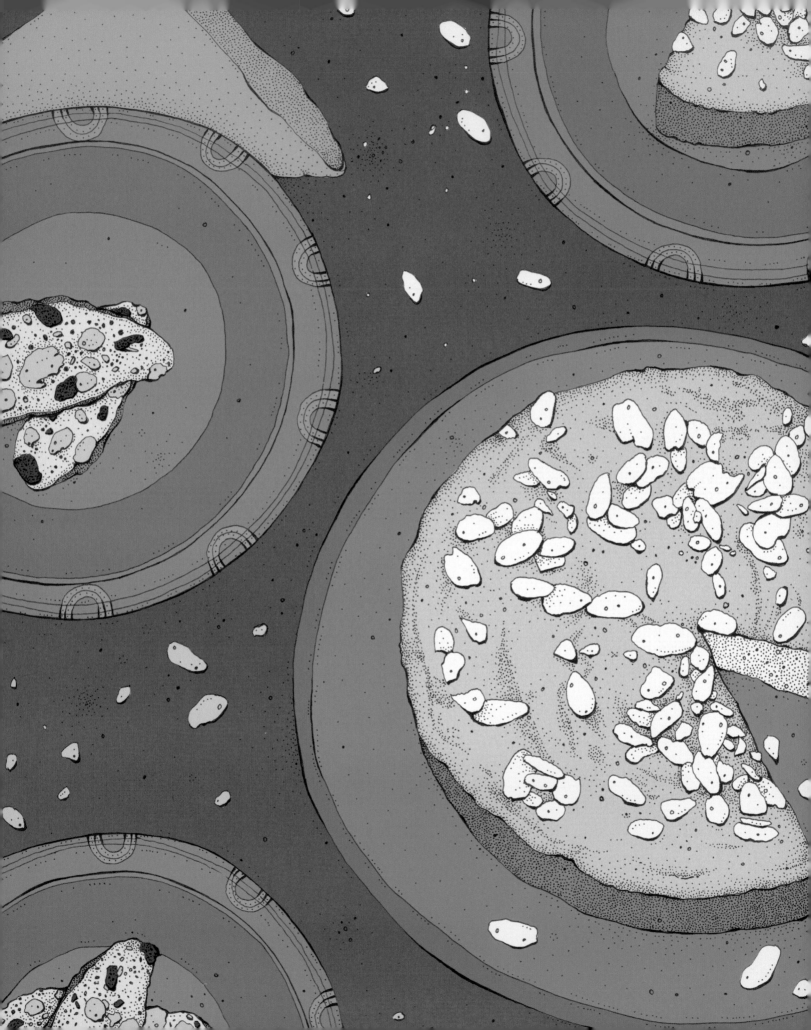

DESSERTS
&
AFTER DINNER

Flourless Chocolate Cake

Preparation time: 20 minutes
Baking time: 35 minutes
Serves 12

A flourless chocolate cake is a real dessert hero, especially when feeding friends who are avoiding wheat. Ground nuts and plenty of chocolate give the cake its structure and a decadently gooey texture within. The espresso bolsters the chocolate flavour rather than adding a coffee taste of its own.

200 g butter, plus extra for greasing

125 g blanched hazelnuts (or ground almonds, see Tip)

200 g light brown soft sugar

200 g dark chocolate, 70% cocoa solids

2 tbsp fresh espresso or 1 tbsp instant coffee granules mixed with 2 tbsp just-boiled water

1 tsp vanilla extract

5 eggs, room temperature

¼ tsp salt

1 tbsp cocoa powder, for dusting

1

Generously grease a 23-cm round springform tin with butter, then line the base with baking parchment. Preheat the oven to 180°C (160°C fan/gas 4). Put the nuts in a food processor with 1 tablespoon of the sugar, then process until finely ground. If using ground almonds, skip this step and add the sugar later on.

NUT OPTIONS
If you can't find pre-skinned (sometimes labelled as blanched) hazelnuts, buy skin-on instead and remove the skins at home. Spread them out in a roasting tin and cook for 8–10 minutes at 180°C (160°C fan/gas 4) until the skins start to crack and look flaky. Tip them into a clean tea towel and rub vigorously to loosen. If a few skins remain attached, don't worry. Let them cool before grinding them. This process will also toast the nuts, giving a rounded and full flavour to your cake. Or, to make the whole process quicker, you could use 125 g ground almonds instead.

2

Break the chocolate into a medium heatproof bowl and add the butter, coffee and vanilla. Melt together gently, either set over a pan of barely simmering water, or in the microwave (see page 119). Stir until smooth, then set aside.

3

Crack the eggs into a large bowl, add the rest of the sugar, then whisk for 5 minutes with an electric mixer until thick, mousse-like and doubled in volume.

4

Pour the melted chocolate around the edge of the bowl (this prevents it from knocking too much air out of the foam). Using a large metal spoon, fold the chocolate in. It might take longer than you expect to get the batter to an almost even brown, and before little ribbons of chocolate stop appearing.

5

Sprinkle the ground nuts and salt into the bowl, then fold them in until evenly blended. Carefully pour the batter into the prepared tin. Preserving the air is the name of the game.

6

Bake on the middle shelf of the oven for about 35 minutes, or until the cake has risen and is set on top, with a just-perceptible wobble underneath the papery crust when you jiggle the tin. Put the tin on a cooling rack as it cools. The torte will sink and crack a little, which is fine.

7

If serving the cake cold, it's easy to transfer it to a plate: just unclip the sides of the tin and use a palette knife to loosen the cake and its lining paper away from the base. To serve warm, leave it in the tin, as the cake is quite delicate. Put the cocoa in a fine-mesh sieve and give the cake a good dusting. Serve with cream or ice cream, and perhaps some berries if you like. The cake can be made up to 2 days ahead (I actually prefer it the next day) and kept in a cool place. Let it come to room temperature before serving.

Tart au Citron

Preparation time: about 1 hour 10
minutes (including blind baking),
plus chilling
Baking time: 5 minutes
Serves 12

I turn to classic lemon tart again and
again for a dessert that works for
just about any meal. The lemon curd
filling is sharp, fresh and citrussy,
and the pastry is a crisp, sweet case
that's simple to make, with no need
to worry about over-mixing. There's
enough pastry for two tarts here, so
put half in the freezer for next time.

For the pastry
1 egg
225 g soft butter
1 tsp vanilla extract
50 g icing sugar, plus extra to
    serve (optional)
½ tsp fine salt
350 g plain flour, plus extra for rolling

For the lemon curd filling
8 eggs
175 g butter
200 g sugar
5 large lemons, juiced (you'll need
    about 250 ml juice)

1

To make the pastry, first separate the egg (see page 127). You will only need the yolk. In a large bowl, beat the butter until it is very soft and smooth. Next, add the egg yolk, vanilla, sugar and salt.

2

Beat together until evenly combined and creamy. Sift in the flour, then work it into the creamed mixture until you have a clumpy but evenly mixed dough, with hardly any dry flour left at the bottom of the bowl.

MAKE IT IN A PROCESSOR
It's very easy to make the pastry by hand, but if you have a food processor, then simply pulse the butter by itself until creamy. Pulse in the yolk, vanilla, sugar and salt, then finish with the flour.

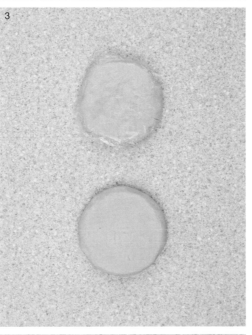

3

Turn out the dough onto the work surface and squish it together to make a smooth ball. It will seem soft, even a bit sticky. Shape into 2 equal-sized discs, then wrap in clingfilm. Chill one piece for at least 30 minutes (you need it to be firm but not hard, or it will crack as it rolls), and reserve the other for another time. It can be frozen for up to 1 month.

4

Preheat the oven to 200°C (180°C fan/gas 6) and use the pastry to line a 23-cm fluted tart tin. Before rolling, flour the work surface and rolling pin. Press shallow ridges across the pastry, then rotate it by a quarter turn. Repeat this until the pastry is about 2 cm thick. If any cracks do appear, pinch them together.

5

Now roll out the pastry to a circle. Roll the pin evenly over the pastry, going forwards and backwards in one direction only. If you roll it in several directions, the pastry is likely to roll unevenly and stretch, which causes shrinking. Turn it by a quarter turn every few rolls, until it is just large enough to line the tin, allowing about a 2.5-cm overhang.

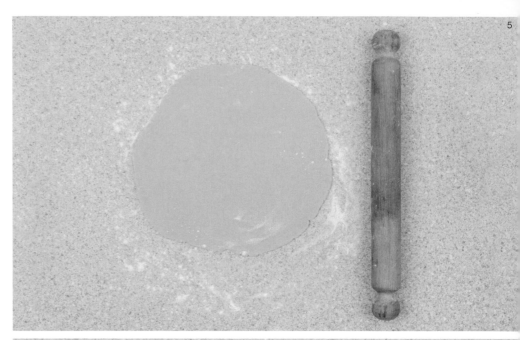

6

Flip the farthest edge of the pastry over the rolling pin, then lift it and carefully drape it over the tin. Taking it a section at a time, gently push the pastry down and into the corner of the tin so it sits at a nice clean right angle. Now pinch off a small ball of excess pastry and use it to press the pastry into the ridges of the tin.

7

Trim the excess pastry away cleanly with a quick roll of the rolling pin across the top of the tin. Pinch the pastry between your finger and thumb so that its edge meets the top of the tin, or better still, comes slightly higher (that way, even if your pastry does shrink, it will still be the same size as the tin). Prick the base all over with a fork, going right down to the metal. Lift onto a baking tray and chill for 10 minutes in the freezer until hard, or longer in the fridge if you have time.

ANY HOLES?

If any holes or tears appear, simply dampen a little piece of the leftover pastry dough and press it into the hole or tear. If cracks appear during baking, smooth a blob of pastry dough over the hot pastry, bake for a few minutes to set, and it will melt and form a delicate seal. Be careful when doing this, though, as too much pressure on the edge of a baked pastry case can cause crumbling – this is for emergency measures only!

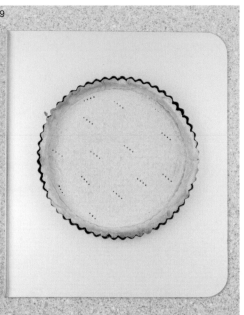

8

When ready to bake, line the pastry with a sheet of foil, making sure all the edges are covered. I tend not to use baking parchment for this, as it can make the pastry sweaty underneath. Fill with baking beans, mounding them up a little at the sides, to support the pastry as it bakes.

9

Bake for 15–20 minutes, or until the pastry looks set and is fairly dry underneath the foil. It should not have taken on much colour at this point. Removing the beans too soon can cause the pastry to sag, so if you're not sure, give it another 5 minutes. Remove the foil and beans from the tin.

10

Turn the oven down to 160°C (140°C fan/gas 3). Bake for another 10–15 minutes, or until the bottom of the pastry is pale gold and feels sandy. If the outside edges are looking brown before the middle of the pastry is ready, carefully wrap in foil and return to the oven.

11

While the pastry is baking, make the filling. Separate 4 eggs (see page 127). You will only need the yolks for this recipe. Beat them with the 4 whole eggs in a large bowl. Cut the butter into small pieces, and put in a heavy-based pan with the sugar and lemon juice.

12
Gently melt the butter and sugar
into the lemon juice. Once melted,
begin to whisk the eggs with one
hand, and simultaneously pour the
hot lemon mixture onto them with
the other. Pour slowly at first so
that the eggs don't get too hot
too quickly, and scramble.

13
Return the mixture to the pan
and cook it over a medium heat for
3–5 minutes, or until thickened and
smooth. Try to avoid letting it boil,
and keep stirring all the time,
concentrating on the edges of
the pan where it is hottest.

14
Pour the lemon curd into the
cooked pastry case, the bake
again for 5 minutes, which just
helps the curd to set.

15
Transfer the tart to a cooling rack,
leave to cool completely, then chill
until ready to serve. Dredge with
icing sugar, if you like.

LEMON MERINGUE PIE
To transform the tart into a lemon
meringue pie, follow the meringue
technique on page 199, beating
4 of the leftover egg whites with
200 g caster sugar. Whisk 1
teaspoon cornflour into the thick
finished meringue. Dollop evenly
over the warm lemon filling, then
spread it up to and slightly over the
pastry edges, peaking the meringue
in dramatic curls as you go. Bake
at 200°C (180°C fan/gas 6) for
20 minutes or until golden, leave to
cool for at least 1 hour, then serve
warm or cold on the day of making.

Strawberry Meringue Cake

Preparation time: 30 minutes
Baking time: about 1 hour
Serves 12

Crisp and fruity, soft and cakey, this playful bake is inspired by the classic Eton mess and makes a great alternative to a pavlova for an unusual summer dessert. Just like Eton mess, the cream is absolutely key to the finished recipe. Pour it lavishly over each portion so it soaks into the cake and mingles with the berries and meringue.

For the cake

110 g butter, plus extra for greasing

4 tbsp double or whipping cream, plus extra to serve

1 tsp vanilla paste, or use extract

250 g ripe strawberries

175 g plain flour

100 g ground almonds

½ tsp baking powder

¼ tsp salt

3 eggs plus 2 yolks

150 g caster sugar

For the topping

2 egg whites

100 g caster sugar

more ripe strawberries, or other summer fruit

1 tbsp icing sugar

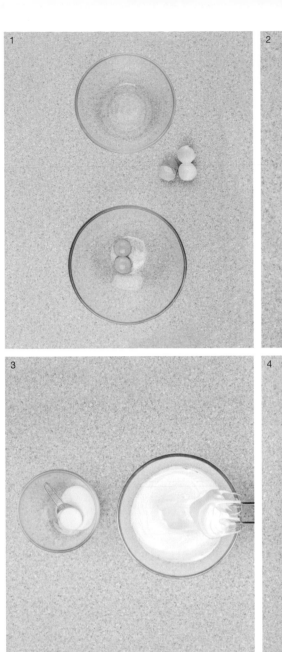

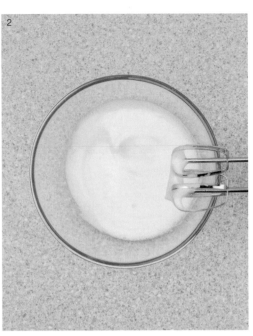

1
Preheat the oven to 180°C (160°C fan/gas 4). Use a little butter to grease a 23-cm round springform cake tin, then line the base with parchment. Get the meringue topping ready first. Separate 2 eggs (see page 127), putting the yolks in a large bowl to use in the cake batter later, and the whites in a separate large bowl.

2
Using an electric mixer, whisk the egg whites until the beaters leave a stiff peak when you pull them away from the bowl. Be careful not to overwhisk them.

3
Add 1 tablespoon of the sugar, then beat until the mixture becomes thick, shiny and holds stiff peaks. Keep adding and whisking back to stiff peaks until all the sugar has been used and the meringue has taken on a pearly sheen.

TOO MUCH EFFORT?
If you like the idea of this cake, but want to reduce the number of steps, simply poke a good handful of crushed ready-made meringue shells into the cake batter before baking.

4
Now for the cake. Melt the butter in a small pan, then remove from the heat and stir in the cream and vanilla. Remove the stems from the strawberries, then cut into fingertip-sized chunks. You should have about 200 g prepared fruit.

5
Mix the flour, ground almonds, baking powder and salt and set aside for later. Crack the 3 whole eggs into the bowl containing the 2 yolks from earlier, then add the caster sugar.

6

Using the electric mixer, beat the eggs and sugar together until doubled in volume, thick and mousse-like, which will take about 5 minutes.

7

Pour the butter mixture into the eggs, whisk briefly, then sift the flour and almond mixture over the top. Whisk briefly again, until evenly blended. Fold in the chopped strawberries, using a large spoon or spatula.

8

Pour the batter into the prepared tin and level the top. Spoon the meringue over the cake to make a sort of crown, with nice pointy peaks if you can. Leave some of the middle of the cake uncovered, as it takes too long to bake otherwise. If the meringue has set a little in the bowl, just fold it a few times with the spoon until smooth.

9

Bake for 10 minutes, then turn the oven down to 160°C (140°C fan/gas 3) and bake for 45–50 minutes more, or until the cake is golden, has risen in the middle and the meringue is crisp and feels dry and hard. Insert a skewer into the middle of the cake to see if it is ready. It will come out clean or just a little sticky when done. Leave to cool for a while in the tin, then carefully unclip it. Leave to cool on a rack, then remove the base and transfer to a serving plate once cooled.

10

Serve the cake with a few more strawberries on top and to the side, with a dusting of icing sugar and a good splash of cream.

Whole Orange & Almond Cake

Preparation time: 10 minutes,
plus 2 hours for boiling the oranges
Baking time: 50 minutes
Serves 12

Whole oranges, skin and all, are
cooked until completely tender,
then blended with almonds, eggs
and a little olive oil in this Spanish-
style, naturally gluten-free cake.
Its texture is light but rich, with a
marmaladey quality.

---

2 medium oranges,
    about 185 g each
2 tbsp extra-virgin olive oil, plus
    extra for greasing
250 g caster sugar
6 eggs, room temperature
300 g ground almonds
1 tbsp baking powder
    (a gluten-free brand if needed)
¼ tsp salt
a handful of flaked almonds
thick Greek yoghurt or crème
    fraîche, to serve (optional)

1
Put the oranges in a medium pan, then cover with water and a lid. Bring to a simmer, then cook for 2 hours, or until the oranges are very soft when you poke them with a knife. The oranges will bob around a bit, so check them after 1 hour and turn them over to make sure they cook evenly. Add more water while you're there, if needed.

ORANGES IN THE MICROWAVE
If you have a microwave, cut the oranges in half (whole ones will explode), put them in a microwave-proof bowl with a splash of water and cover with clingfilm. Pierce a few holes in the film. Cook on full power for 10 minutes, or until completely tender (it may take longer, depending on your microwave). Leave to cool for a few minutes before removing the film.

2
Grease a 23-cm round springform tin with a little oil, then line with baking parchment. Preheat the oven to 180°C (160°C fan/gas 4). Drain the oranges, and when cool enough to handle, cut into large pieces and remove any pips. Put them, skin and all, in a food processor. Add the sugar and pulse to a smooth purée.

3
Add the eggs to the processor, then whizz for about 1 minute until paler and thickened.

4

Tip in the ground almonds, baking powder, salt and oil and process for a few seconds to make a smooth, evenly blended batter. Using a spatula, scrape the batter into the prepared tin, smooth the top, then scatter with the flaked almonds.

5

Bake for 50 minutes, or until the cake is golden all over and has risen all the way to the centre, and a skewer inserted in the middle comes out clean. Remove and leave to cool in the tin for 10 minutes (the cake will sink back down to become flat), then run a palette knife between the cake and the tin and unclip the sides. Leave the cake to cool on the tin base, on a cooling rack.

6

There's a trick to getting a cake with a loose topping onto a plate without any dramas. Put a flat plate upside-down on top of the cake. Holding the plate and the tin securely, turn them both over. Remove the tin and baking parchment. Put a serving plate on top upside-down, then, holding both plates securely but without squashing the cake, turn it the right way up. Serve with thick Greek yoghurt or crème fraîche.

Chocolate Profiteroles

Preparation time: 20 minutes
Baking time: 30 minutes per batch
Serves 6 (makes 18)

Once you've discovered how easy it is to make choux pastry at home, you'll be making profiteroles again and again. Cooled, unfilled choux buns will keep in an airtight container for 3 days or freeze for 1 month. Refresh in a hot oven to crisp them up, then continue from step 8.

For the pastry

125 g plain flour

1 tsp sugar

a pinch of salt

85 g butter, plus extra for greasing

240 ml water

3 eggs

For the chocolate sauce

200 g dark chocolate, 60–70% cocoa solids, broken into pieces

150 ml double cream

100 ml milk

1 tsp vanilla paste or extract

a pinch of salt

For the filling

450 ml double cream

2 tbsp icing sugar

½ tsp vanilla paste or extract

1

For the pastry, first sift the flour, sugar and salt together onto a piece of baking parchment.

2

Put the butter and water in a medium pan. Heat over a fairly low heat until the butter has completely melted. Once melted, increase the heat and bring the water to a rolling boil. Keep a wooden spoon on hand. With the pan still on the stove, and using the baking parchment like a chute, quickly pour the flour mixture into the pan, then grab the wooden spoon and start mixing it vigorously. Turn off the heat. It will seem weirdly lumpy at first, but keep beating. You need to add the flour quickly after the water comes to the boil, to avoid letting too much of it evaporate.

3

After a short period of beating, the lumpy batter will transform into a shiny, thick smooth paste that comes away cleanly from the edge of the pan. Stop beating.

4

Spoon the paste onto a cold plate and spread it out with the wooden spoon. This helps to cool it quickly. When it's barely warm to the touch, move on to step 5.

5

Beat the eggs together in a measuring jug. Put the paste in a large bowl, then add the egg in small additions, beating until fully incorporated each time. The paste will get stiffer, then looser. You can do this with an electric mixer if you prefer. Stop adding egg when the mixture is smooth and silky, and falls in a smooth dollop from the spoon when shaken sharply. The paste can be chilled for up to a day at this point.

6

When ready to bake, preheat the oven to 220°C (200°C fan/gas 7). Grease then line 2 large baking trays with baking parchment. Spoon 18 heaped teaspoons pastry onto the trays, aiming for walnut-sized balls. If you want to be neat, pipe the pastry onto the trays using a 1-cm nozzle and a large piping bag. Smooth any points with a wet finger.

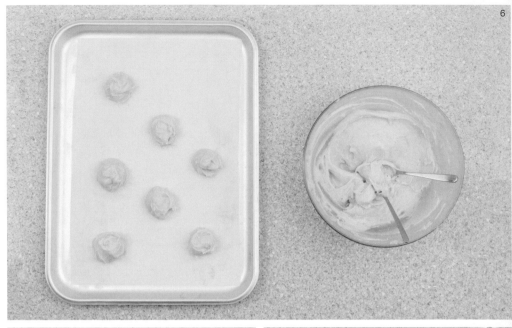

7

Bake for 10 minutes, then turn down the oven to 200°C (180°C fan/gas 6) and cook for 20 minutes, or until very crisp and golden brown. The pastry should hardly give at all when gently squeezed. It's best to bake in batches, but if you need to, bake 2 trays at a time. Don't open the oven door to turn the trays around until the pastry has risen well and is changing colour, or they will deflate. Once cooked, cut each profiterole widthways, but not all the way through, then bake for 5 minutes more. This lets the steam out from the centres and will help keep the pastry crisper for longer. Remove and leave to cool.

8

To make the sauce, chop the chocolate. Bring the cream and milk to a simmer, add the chocolate, vanilla and salt, then remove from the heat and stir until smooth and silky. It can be made ahead and warmed gently when ready to serve.

9

Profiteroles are best filled shortly before serving, but you can fill them 2 hours ahead and store them in the fridge. Put the cream, sugar and vanilla in a large bowl and whip until thickened, but not stiff. Spoon it generously into the cold profiteroles.

10

Pour the warm chocolate sauce over them to serve.

One-Crust Apple & Blackberry Pie

Preparation time: 25 minutes,
plus chilling (if making own pastry)
Baking time: 35–50 minutes
Serves 8

This is the most democratic of pies,
and needs no special equipment.
A simple, sturdy but tender pastry
crust holds the juicy contents inside
(or you can use 350 g ready-made
dough). Try using rhubarb and
strawberries or perhaps peaches
and blueberries once you've got
the hang of it.

For the sweet shortcrust pastry
200 g plain flour, plus extra for rolling
¼ tsp salt
50 g cold vegetable shortening
    or lard
70 g cold butter
1 egg
2 tbsp sugar

For the filling
650 g tangy dessert apples
    (about 3–4)
1 lemon, or 1 tbsp lemon juice
    from a bottle
2 tbsp cornflour
½ tsp ground cinnamon or nutmeg
100 g blackberries, fresh or frozen
    and defrosted (or other soft,
    sharp fruit)
100 g sugar
2 tbsp semolina or fine cornmeal
1 tbsp demerara sugar
1 tbsp butter

1

Make the pastry first. Sift the flour into a large bowl and add the salt. Cut the shortening and butter into cubes, then add to the bowl. Separate the egg and beat the yolk with 2 tablespoons water. Reserve the egg white for later on.

2

Rub the fat into the flour with your hands until the mixture resembles fine crumbs, then stir in the sugar. A food processor makes light work of this job, if you have one.

3

Splash the egg yolk and water over the rubbed-in mixture, then quickly work it in using a table knife until it comes together. If using a processor, process until the pastry comes together to a smooth ball. Try to avoid adding any more liquid, or mixing it too much once the dough starts to take shape. If the dough really won't come together, add 1 teaspoon more water. Some flours are drier than others, so the amount of liquid you need can vary.

4

If making by hand, knead the dough briefly to make a smooth ball. Shape into a disc, wrap in clingfilm and chill for 30 minutes, or until firm but not rock hard, while you prepare the filling. Preheat the oven to 190°C (170°C fan/gas 5). Put a baking sheet in the oven to heat up. This will provide a boost of heat to the bottom of the pastry and help it crisp up.

5

Peel the apples, chop the flesh away from the cores in big chunks, then slice them thinly. Toss in a large bowl with 1 tablespoon lemon juice, the cornflour, spice and berries. Don't add the sugar yet, as it can make the fruit a little wet by the time the pastry is ready.

6

Cut a large square of baking parchment and sprinkle it lightly with flour. Using a floured rolling pin, press ridges evenly across the pastry. Rotate the pastry and paper by a quarter turn and repeat. Do this until the pastry is about 1 cm thick. If any cracks appear at the edges, pinch them back together.

7

Roll the pastry out into a 30-cm round. Roll forwards and back, not side to side, and turn the pastry and paper a quarter turn every few rolls. This will help the pastry stretch without becoming tough.

8

Slide the pastry, still on its paper, onto a baking tray. Sprinkle the semolina or cornmeal over the middle. Toss the sugar into the fruit, then mound it in the middle of the pastry, leaving a border of about 7 cm. Lightly beat the egg white with a fork, then brush it around the edges with a pastry brush.

9

Push the pastry up and around the fruit, pinching it here and there to make a sort of basket shape. If any cracks appear, just pinch the pastry together to re-seal. Dot the butter over the fruit. Brush the outside of the pastry with the egg white and scatter with demerara sugar.

10

Slide the baking tray on top of the preheated baking sheet. Bake for 35–40 minutes, or until golden and crisp and the apples are just tender. If they are not quite cooked but the pastry is, reduce the temperature to 180°C (160°C fan/gas 4) and give it 10 more minutes. Cool for at least 10 minutes to let the juices settle, then serve hot or warm with ice cream, cream or custard.

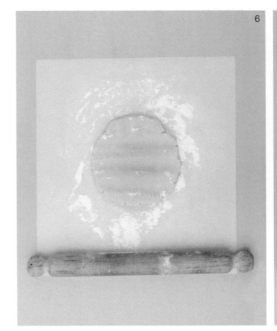
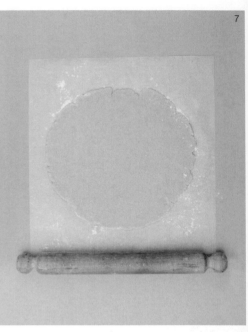

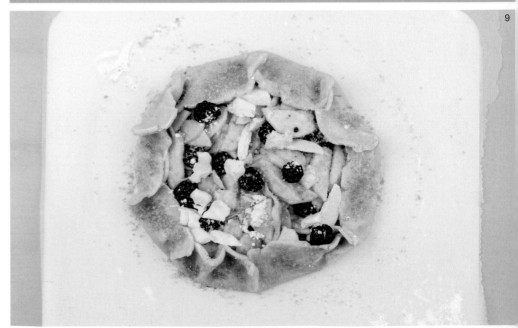

Upside-Down Fruit Cake

Preparation time: 20 minutes
Baking time: 55 minutes–1 hour
Makes 12 slices

I love the way that despite its glossy
looks, this is a down-to-earth bake,
ready to change with the seasons
as they roll round. Cherries, apricots,
peaches, apples, pears, even the
classic pineapple will happily meld
into the bottom of the rich almond
sponge. Serve slightly warm with
soured cream or crème fraiche, or
a jug of custard if it's cold outside.

For the cake

250 g soft butter, plus extra
    for greasing
250 g light brown soft sugar
140 g plain flour
2 tsp baking powder
¼ tsp salt
100 g ground almonds
125 g soured cream or crème fraîche
4 eggs, room temperature
½ tsp almond extract

For the fruit

8–10 firmish ripe plums
4 tbsp light brown soft sugar

1
Preheat the oven to 180°C (160°C fan/gas 4). Use a little butter to grease a 23-cm round springform tin, then line the base with baking parchment. Halve and stone the plums, then cut each half into 3 wedges. Toss them with the 4 tablespoons light brown sugar.

2
Arrange the fruit in the bottom of the tin in neat rings, if you have time, or be more rustic. They must be in a single layer. Make sure you add all the sugar.

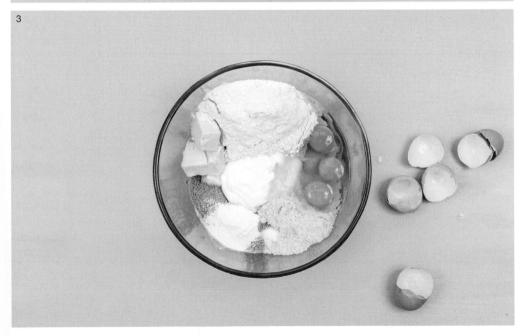

3
For the cake, put the butter in a large mixing bowl with the dry ingredients, soured cream or crème fraîche, eggs and almond extract.

4
Use an electric mixer to beat everything to a smooth, fairly thick cake batter.

5
Spoon the batter on top of the fruit, then smooth the top.

6
Bake for 55 minutes–1 hour, or until the cake is golden and has risen; a skewer should come out clean when inserted into the middle. Run a palette knife around the edge of the tin to loosen the cake, then leave to cool on a cooling rack.

7
Serve the cake warm. If you need to reheat it, cover it loosely with foil and let it warm through in a low oven for 15 minutes.

PEAR & CHOCOLATE CAKE
Toss 450 g sliced just-ripe pears with the sugar. Add 100 g dark chocolate chips to the cake batter.

PINEAPPLE CAKE
Toss 450 g pineapple chunks (drained if tinned) with the sugar. For a really retro touch, poke glacé cherries here and there between the fruit.

SPICED APPLE CARAMEL CAKE
Toss 450 g sliced, peeled apples with the sugar. Mix 2 teaspoons ground mixed spice in with the flour. Drizzle with ready-made caramel sauce or dulce de leche to serve.

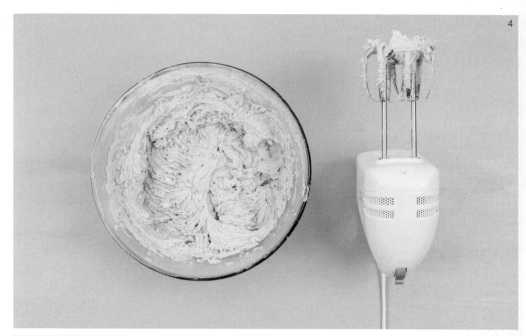

Classic Baked Cheesecake

Preparation time: 20 minutes,
plus chilling
Baking time: 55 minutes
Cuts into 12 generous slices,
more if you need it to

Creamy and cool, with a crisp base
with just a hint of ginger, this baked
cheesecake is sweet but not cloying.
The cooling time is all-important,
so make this the last thing you do
in the kitchen on the day you make
it. Serve with seasonal fruit, or pale
and interesting, all by itself.

For the base

110 g soft butter

250 g digestive biscuits

2 tbsp caster sugar

½ tsp ground ginger (optional)

For the filling

900 g full-fat cream cheese,
    at room temperature

200 g caster sugar

1 tbsp cornflour

1 vanilla pod or 1 tsp vanilla paste

1 lemon

5 eggs, room temperature

250 g full-fat crème fraîche

1

Preheat the oven to 200°C (180°C fan/gas 6). Melt the butter in a medium pan, then use a little to grease a 23-cm round springform tin. Line the base with a circle of baking parchment. Crush the biscuits until fine and sandy. You can do this by putting them in a strong plastic food storage bag, squishing out the air, then whacking them with a rolling pin. Or use a food processor, as I have here.

2

Mix the melted butter, 2 tablespoons sugar, and the ginger, if using, into the crumbs, until evenly blended and rather like wet sand. Press into the base of the tin, spreading firmly with the back of a spoon, until evenly spread.

3

Put the tin on a baking tray, then bake for 10 minutes, or until golden. Leave to cool.

4

To make the filling, put the cream cheese and sugar in a large bowl, then sift the cornflour over it. If using a vanilla pod, split it in half lengthways and scrape out the seeds. Finely grate the zest from the lemon, and add the vanilla and lemon zest to the bowl. Using a spatula, beat until smooth. A spatula is better than a whisk here because you don't want to beat in too much air, which can cause cracks.

5

Separate 2 of the eggs (see page 127), saving the whites for another time. Beat the 3 whole eggs and 2 yolks into the cheese mixture one by one, until very smooth.

6

Finish by beating in 125 g crème fraîche. Pour the mixture onto the crumb crust, then level the top.

7

Bake for 10 minutes, then turn the oven down to 150°C (130°C fan/gas 2) and bake for another 45 minutes, or until the middle wobbles slightly as you jiggle the tin, and the top has turned very pale gold at the edges. Check the cake after two thirds of the baking time and give it a turn if needed. When it's ready, loosen the edge of the cake from the tin using a palette knife, then return to the turned-off oven and leave it to cool in the oven with the door ajar for 1 hour. Remove and leave to cool to room temperature for a couple of hours, then chill overnight.

8

For optimal creaminess, take the cheesecake from the fridge half an hour before you want to eat it. Smooth the rest of the crème fraîche over the top, then serve.

Mint-Chocolate
Macarons

Preparation time: 25 minutes,
plus drying and settling time
Baking time: 12 minutes per batch
Makes 18–20 sandwiched macarons

Anyone can make home-made
macarons – with just a few pieces
of kitchen equipment, they're
more of a pleasure than a challenge,
and make a special after-dinner bite
or a perfect gift. They need time to
dry and set, so relax into making
them and stagger the recipe around
your day.

For the basic macaron batter

100 g ground almonds

100 g icing sugar

3 eggs (whites only)

a pinch of salt

100 g caster sugar

green food colouring paste (optional)

For the mint-chocolate filling

100 g dark chocolate,
   either 60 or 70% cocoa solids

½ tsp mint extract

120 ml double cream

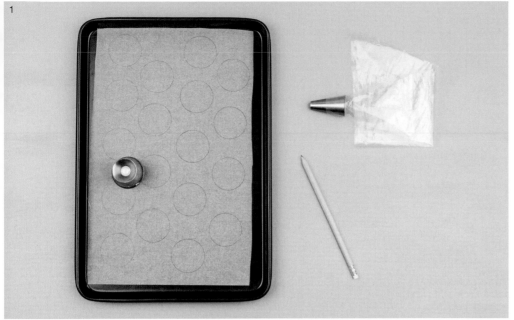

1
Prepare 2 heavy baking trays:
line them with non-stick baking
parchment, then draw 20 x 4.5-cm
circles on each tray, allowing about
2.5 cm of space around each circle.
I use an egg cup, but a small pastry
cutter or an upturned shot glass
should be about right too. Fit a
piping bag with a 1-cm plain nozzle.

WHICH BAKING TRAY?
Dark, heavy metal baking trays
give better results than lighter
silver ones, creating more perfectly
Parisian 'feet' (a little skirt of
bubbles) on the bottom of the
macarons. Use your sturdiest
baking tray or tin.

2
Put the ground almonds and
icing sugar in the bowl of a food
processor and pulse until the
almonds are very fine – about
30 seconds. I find that the sugar
sinks to the bottom of the bowl,
so after 15 seconds or so, give
everything a stir and process again.
Sift the mixture and discard any
larger pieces of almond that remain.

3
Separate the eggs (see page 127)
and measure the whites: you will
need exactly 100 g. Then, in a
very clean large bowl and using an
electric mixer, beat the whites with
the salt until stiff, but not dry or
fluffy around the edges.

4

Add 1 tablespoon of the caster sugar, then beat again until the mixture returns to stiff peaks. Do this repeatedly until all the sugar has been used, and you have a thick, glossy bowl of meringue that looks rather like shaving foam.

5

Add a few dabs of of the food colouring, if using, and whisk again until evenly green. Food colourings go a long way and you can always add more, so go easy to begin with until you reach the colour you want.

6

Fold the sifted almond and sugar mixture into the meringue. If at this point the meringue is still very thick and fluffy, the macarons can turn out a little rougher-looking on the top when baked. If this is the case, break the meringue-making rules and beat the mixture a little with a spatula until it loosens ever so slightly. Transfer half the mixture to the piping bag, taking care not to create too many pockets of air.

PIPING KNOW-HOW
Filling a piping bag is much easier if you first open the bag out over your left hand if you are right handed (or vice versa), or over a tall glass or jam jar. You can then fill the bag no more than half full before flipping the top of the bag back over and twisting the top to create the pressure needed to pipe.

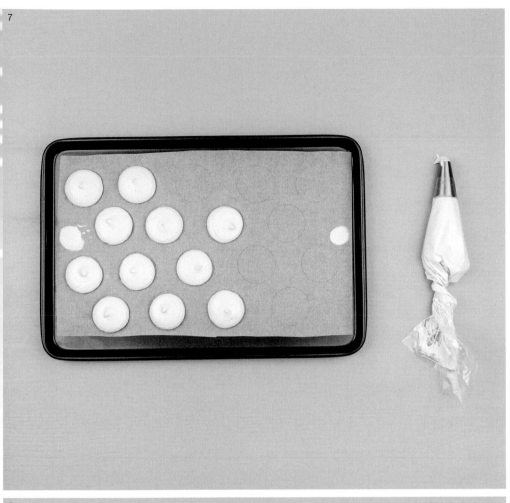

7

Before you pipe, be sure to turn the paper over to avoid having pencil marks on the bottom of your macarons. Secure the paper to the baking trays with a small dot of the meringue at either end. Pipe the mixture onto the marked circles, keeping the bag upright, starting in the middle of the circle, and then squeezing with an even pressure. Let the batter ooze out in one continuous flow until it almost reaches the pencil lines, then stop squeezing and lift the nozzle away. Gently press any points down with your finger (don't wet it), if you need to. You should get between 36 and 40 circles.

8

Leave the macarons to dry for 1 hour, to let a skin form over the top. It's best if you don't cook anything else steamy in the kitchen at the same time. The batter should not stick to your finger when touched lightly. Preheat the oven to 160°C (140°C fan/gas 3).

9

Bake the macarons, one tray at a time, for 12 minutes, or until they have risen on little bubbly platforms, and look shiny on top. Try to avoid letting them turn golden; turn the tray halfway through if they look uneven. Once cooked, carefully pull the paper, complete with macarons, off the baking tray and leave to cool on a flat work surface.

10

To make the filling, chop the chocolate and put it in a heatproof bowl with the mint extract. Bring the cream to the boil in a small pan, then pour this over the chocolate. Allow to melt, stirring every now and again, to make a smooth ganache.

11

When the ganache is cool, thick and glossy, sandwich the macarons together. Spoon about 1 teaspoon of the ganache on top of the flat sides of half of the macarons. Gently sandwich with the other halves. The chocolate will ooze out to the edges.

12

Leave the filling to set completely. Keep the macarons in a cool place until serving.

PISTACHIO MACARONS
Grind 50 g shelled pistachios in the processor. Add 50 g ground almonds and the icing sugar, process, then follow as before. Sandwich with chocolate ganache, leaving out the mint extract.

RASPBERRY MACARONS
Colour the mixture with pink food colouring paste. Sandwich the macarons with 1 teaspoon best-quality raspberry jam.

Pistachio & Fig Biscotti

Preparation time: 20 minutes
Baking time: 1 hour
Makes about 36 biscotti

It's easy to make your own elegant biscotti, baked twice for just the right crunch, ready for dunking into coffee or sweet dessert wine after dinner, or crumbling over ice cream. I've chosen figs and pistachio, for flavour and their graphic, colourful cross-section, but any combination of dried fruit and nuts will work brilliantly.

---

2 tbsp olive oil, plus a little extra
   for greasing
100 g soft dried figs
   (or other dried fruit)
200 g caster sugar
3 eggs, room temperature
300 g plain flour, plus extra
   for dusting
1 tsp baking powder
½ tsp salt
1 orange
100 g shelled pistachios

1
Grease and line a large baking tray with baking parchment. Preheat the oven to 180°C (160°C fan/gas 4). Snip or cut the figs into small pieces.

2
Put the sugar and eggs in a large bowl, then whisk for a minute or so with a balloon whisk, just until the mixture feels frothy and a little more resistant as you beat. Whisk in the oil.

3
Mix the flour, baking powder and salt, then sift them over the egg mixture. Fold together to make a dough. Finely grate the zest from the orange, then work it into the dough along with the nuts and figs, using a spatula.

4
Scatter some flour on the work surface and turn the dough out onto it. Split the dough into 2 equal balls, dust each one (and your hands) with a little flour, then shape into a 20–25-cm sausage. The dough is quite soft, so be gentle with it, and pat it into shape rather than squeezing it too much. Lift it onto the prepared baking tray.

5
Bake for 30 minutes, or until they have risen and turned pale golden. Leave to cool, and in the meantime turn the oven down to 160°C (140°C fan/gas 3).

6
When the dough is firm and cool enough to handle, transfer the biscotti to a board and cut into 1-cm slices. Use a serrated knife and sawing action, as the dough is quite sturdy by this point. Spread the cookies over the baking tray in a single layer. Use a second tray if you want to bake all the cookies at once.

GETTING AHEAD
The half-baked biscotti can be frozen at this point and baked from frozen when needed. Allow a few more minutes of baking time.

7
Return the biscotti to the oven and bake for another 30 minutes, turning them over halfway through, until dry, crisp and just golden. If you are baking 2 trays at once, swap their shelf positions halfway through cooking too.

8
Cool the biscotti on a rack, then pack in an airtight container until serving. They will last up to 2 weeks.

SPICED PECAN-CRANBERRY BISCOTTI
Sift 2 teaspoons ground mixed spice into the flour. Replace the pistachios and figs with pecans and cranberries.

ANISE & ALMOND BISCOTTI
Work in whole blanched almonds instead of the pistachios, and add 1 teaspoon lightly crushed anise or fennel seeds.

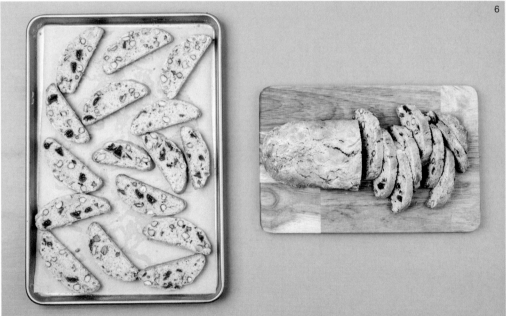

Salted Caramel Shortbread Bites

Preparation time: 45 minutes,
plus setting
Baking time: 25–30 minutes
Makes 36 small cubes

If you're a fan of the salt and
caramel combination but haven't
tried it at home yet, this is a delicious
way to experiment. The recipe is
a twist on millionaire's shortbread,
a classic childhood favourite of
mine. It's now all grown up, and
perfect as a bite after dinner.

For the base

110 g soft butter, plus extra
   for greasing
50 g caster sugar
a pinch of flaky sea salt
½ tsp vanilla extract
140 g plain flour

For the caramel

110 g butter
200 g dark brown soft sugar
4 tbsp golden syrup
½ tsp flaky sea salt
1 x 400-g tin full-fat condensed milk

For the topping

200 g dark chocolate,
   70% cocoa solids
1 tbsp vegetable or sunflower oil
½ tsp flaky sea salt

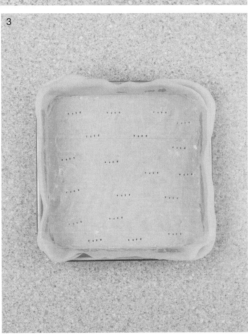

1

Lightly grease a 23-cm shallow square baking tin, then line with baking parchment. Make the base first. Put the butter in a large bowl and beat well with a wooden spoon or an electric mixer until creamy and very pale. Add the sugar, salt and vanilla and beat again until even paler.

2

Sift the flour over the creamed butter and sugar. Using a spatula, gently work the flour into the mixture to make an even dough that starts to clump together.

3

Press the dough into the prepared tin, then level and smooth it with the back of a spoon. Prick it all over with a fork, then chill for 10 minutes, or longer if you like, until firm. Meanwhile, preheat the oven to 160°C (140°C fan/gas 3).

4

Bake for 25–30 minutes, or until the shortbread is golden all over. Leave to cool completely.

QUICK SHORTCUT

If you prefer, buy 400 g ready-made all-butter shortbread biscuits. Crush them finely, then stir in 4 tablespoons melted butter until even. Press into the tin, bake for 15 minutes, or until golden, then continue with the recipe.

5

Now for the caramel. Melt the butter, sugar, syrup and salt together gently in a pan, then stir in the condensed milk.

6

Bring the caramel to a simmer, stirring constantly with a spatula, and let it bubble for 4 minutes, or until it thickens and smells like creamy toffee. It should be thick enough for the spatula to leave a trail in the caramel for a few seconds. Don't leave the pan or stop stirring during this step, as it can easily burn on the base.

7

Pour the caramel over the shortbread, then leave to cool completely.

8

Once the caramel has set and cooled, it's time to finish the layers. Melt the chocolate either over a pan of water or in the microwave (see page 119), stir in the oil, then pour this over the caramel. Sprinkle with the salt and leave to set at room temperature, or in the fridge if it's a hot day. The oil helps stop the chocolate setting too hard, which can make it difficult to cut.

9

When the chocolate is just set, mark it into squares (I use a ruler to get the lines perfectly straight), then chill until completely firm.

10

Cut into cubes to serve. For a really clean finish, wipe the blade of your knife with a slightly damp cloth between each slice. Store in an airtight container for up to 3 days.

MILLIONAIRE'S SHORTBREAD
To make classic millionaire's shortbread, simply reduce the salt to a pinch in the caramel, and omit it from the top too.

What to Bake

If you're still not sure what to bake for a particular occasion or need, how about a few of these suggestions?

No time to bake?
Fruity Cupcakes, 26
Favourite Swiss Roll, 38
Victoria Sandwich
   (using all-in-one method), 46
Chocolate & Nut Banana Bread, 50
Malted Milk Chocolate
   Birthday Cake, 64
Carrot Cake with Cream Cheese
   Frosting (as cupcakes), 92
Skinny Blueberry Muffins, 104

Bake-sale bestsellers
Golden Citrus Drizzle Cake, 22
Malted Milk Chocolate Birthday
   Cake (without the candles), 64
Cherry-Almond Streusel Slice, 88
Buttermilk Pound Cake
   (lemon flavour), 30
Carrot Cake with Cream
   Cheese Frosting (whole or
   as cupcakes), 92
Caramel & Walnut Coffee Cake, 110
Jaffa Marble Loaf, 84

Baking with children
Peanut Butter Cookies, 34
Fruity Cupcakes, 26
Iced Gingerbread Cookies, 42
Lemon & Raisin Pancakes, 52
Favourite Swiss Roll, 38
Skinny Blueberry Muffins, 104
Red Velvet Whoopie Pies
   (banoffee variation), 164

Children's birthday parties
Rocky Road, 56
Fruity Cupcakes, 26
Malted Milk Chocolate
   Birthday Cake, 64
Peanut Butter Cookies
   or Seriously Chocolatey
   Cookies (as ice-cream
   sandwiches), 34/118

Bake ahead & freeze
Jaffa Marble Loaf, 84
Victoria Sandwich, 46
Chocolate Fudge Layer Cake, 134
Seriously Chocolatey Cookies, 118
Peanut Butter Cookies, 34
Cranberry Stollen, 182

Picnics & camping
Blueberry-Cinnamon
   Crumb Cake, 114
Golden Citrus Drizzle Cake, 22
Rocky Road, 56
Whole Orange & Almond Cake, 202
Salted Caramel Shortbread Bites, 232
Jaffa Marble Loaf, 84
Buttermilk Pound Cake, 30
Chocolate & Nut Banana Bread, 50

Baby shower
Frosted Cupcakes (use baby blue
   and pink or yellow colouring), 160
Mint-Chocolate Macarons
   (raspberry variation), 22
Fudgy Cheesecake Brownies, 96
Linzer Cookies (sandwiched
   with lemon curd), 138

Wedding, anniversary or formal party
Vanilla Celebration Cake, 168
Festive Fruit Cake, 176
Frosted Cupcakes, 160
Chocolate Fudge Layer Cake, 134

Classic English afternoon tea party
Classic Crusty Bread (made
   into cucumber sandwiches), 68
Vanilla Fruit Scones (with cream
   and jam), 60
Classic Shortbread, 76
Tart au Citron (cut into
   small pieces), 192

Valentine's Day
Red Velvet Whoopie Pies, 164
Fudgy Cheesecake Brownies
   (swirl the topping in heart shapes), 96
Mint-Chocolate Macarons
   (raspberry variation), 222
Classic Shortbread
   (lavender variation), 76

Easter
Chocolate Fudge Layer Cake
   (topped with chocolate eggs), 134
Chocolate Hazelnut Log (decorate
   with chicks, chocolate eggs
   and spring flowers), 172
Festive Fruit Cake, 176

Mother's Day
Blueberry-Cinnamon
   Crumb Cake, 114
Coconut Layer Cake, 142
Classic Baked Cheesecake, 218
Lemon-Glazed Ginger Cake, 100
Angel Cake with Berries, 152
Vanilla Celebration Cake, 168
Chocolate Fudge Layer Cake, 134
Strawberry Meringue Cake, 198

Halloween
Red Velvet Whoopie Pies
   (pumpkin variation), 164
Malted Milk Chocolate Birthday
   Cake (graveyard variation), 64
Easy Baked Doughnuts, 126
Linzer Cookies (vampire-style;
   puncture two holes in the top
   cookies to let the jam
   ooze through), 138

Christmas
Festive Fruit Cake, 176
Cranberry Stollen, 182
Sticky Pear & Pecan Toffee Cake, 156
Chocolate Hazelnut Log, 172
Linzer Cookies, 138
Pistachio & Fig Biscotti (spiced
   pecan cranberry variation), 228

Index

With thanks

I couldn't have made this book without the help and support from these wonderful people. For the photos, Liz and Max Haarala Hamilton, thank you for all your spirit, creativity, and the gorgeous shots, and Ruth Carruthers for lightening their load. Thanks also to my assistants Sophie Austen-Smith, Hannah Sherwood and Lucy Campbell for keeping the cakes a-coming, and not to forget Teresa Coen and my wonderful mum Linda for stepping in and saving the day.

Thanks to Leslie Hutchings for your advice and to my heroic recipe testers, Mum (again), Pip Bennett, Helen Barker-Benfield, Germaine McBride, Lucy Campbell, Pauline Copestake, Catherine Gardner, Sarah Goss and Emma Henry for baking my recipes in your own kitchens.

To the all of the Phaidon team, but most especially Emma Robertson for kicking this whole thing off, and to Laura Gladwin for taking it through to the finish line. Thanks to Kerry Lemon for her brilliant, stand-out illustrations, Ana Minguez for her careful design work, and Kathy Steer for her keen eye on the proofs. Grateful thanks to Magimix UK for help with equipment.

Finally, to Ross, for all your belief and support, and all our friends, family and neighbours, who've eaten the contents of this book three times over. We made this together, everyone; thank you from the bottom of my heart.

Note on the recipes

Some recipes include raw or very lightly cooked eggs. These should be avoided by the elderly, infants, pregnant women, convalescents and anyone with an impaired immune system.

Phaidon Press Limited
Regent's Wharf
All Saints Street
London N1 9PA

www.phaidon.com

© 2014 Phaidon Press Limited

ISBN 978 0 7148 6743 4

A CIP catalogue record is available from the British Library.

Commissioning Editor: Emma Robertson
Project Editor: Laura Gladwin
Production Controller: Mandy Mackie

Photographs by Liz and Max Haarala Hamilton
Illustrations by Kerry Lemon
Design concept by SML Office
Artwork by Ana Minguez

Printed in China